THE INVE$TORS GUIDE TO

GROWING WEALTH
IN
SELF STORAGE

The Step-by-Step Playbook for Turning a Real Estate Asset Into a Thriving Self Storage Business

AJ Osborne

Founder of Keylock Storage
Host of *Self Storage Income* Podcast

The Investors Guide to Growing Wealth in Self Storage
How to Turn a Real Estate Asset Into a Thriving Business
By AJ Osborne © 2020

Print ISBN: 978-1-7352588-0-5
eBook ISBN: 978-1-7352588-1-2
PDF eBook ISBN: 978-1-7352588-2-9

Interior Design by: Fusion Creative Works, FusionCW.com
Cover Design by: Mirko Pohle
Lead Editor: Jennifer Regner

For more information, visit SelfStorageIncome.com

Book Production by Aloha Publishing

Published by

Printed in the United States of America

This book is dedicated to my partners, Ron Osborne and Sam Whitaker. This book represents our cumulative knowledge, not just mine. Without my partners, it would not exist.

I also dedicate this to every person on our staff, who have all helped us every step of the way.

CONTENTS

INTRODUCTION

I opened my eyes. It was bright—must be in the afternoon. I was glad it wasn't night; the nights were confusing and scary to me. It was the pain that woke me—it was always the pain. It was relentless, moving from terrible to excruciating. The nurses were going in and out as my mom and wife sat, talking and playing with my new 5-month-old son, Theo.

My mouth was so dry it felt like it was cracking. I hadn't had water in weeks, and it felt like years. Time had become a strange concept to me, and I was not sure of the day or month. I was not even sure how long I had been there. The pain became more intense so I moved my head up and down, trying to get someone's attention.

Not that there was anything they could do. I wanted to scream, but I had long lost my ability to speak or do anything else on my own. Tubes ran in and out of my body. My body had even lost the ability to keep itself alive. I was paralyzed from head to toe. As if being paralyzed wasn't enough, the pain was overwhelming: every inch of my body suffered. My skin felt like it was on fire, a 24-hour burn. The weight of my own body felt like it was crushing my bones. I lay naked in the bed because even the weight of a light sheet was too much to bear.

For what seemed like an eternity, every morning I opened my eyes and was surprised that I wasn't dead. Many times, I wished I was. Every waking hour was a fight, one that I did not know how to win.

I was moved from hospital to hospital. They eventually sent me to a facility that would keep me on life support with no known checkout date. Because my eyes were partially paralyzed, I could only see to the end of my bed. It was impossible for me to know where I was. The nurses came in and out, checking on vitals and tending to me. They would roll my lifeless body over to bathe me by wiping my body down.

I was not always like this. I am a father of four who loves the outdoors: hiking, skiing, fly-fishing, and anything else that would get me into the mountains. I was 33 when, one night, I started to feel pain in my legs. That night we went to the ER, but they sent me home because there was "nothing wrong" with me. They said I was perfectly healthy.

Within hours, my legs stopped working. No one could figure out what was happening. Within days, I went from being fit enough to run several miles to not being able to breathe. The last thing I remember before medical professionals put me under was my wife telling me they were going to get me help and stop the pain. When I opened my eyes, I was on life support, paralyzed from head to toe.

But I survived and slowly started getting better. As you can imagine, becoming paralyzed from head to toe and living on life support can create some challenges in life. Challenges that do not have answers—something I was growing accustomed to. Will I walk again? We don't know. Will I be able to go home next month? We don't know. Will the pain end? We don't know. By this time, I was just happy I could speak. I had been on tubes for so long that every little thing was a miracle to me. It had been months since I had gone into the hospital and did not know when I would leave. I didn't even get to say good-bye to my children.

Before this breakdown happened, I worked for a national insurance brokerage company. I had always been in sales. My father worked in the insurance industry and I followed in his footsteps. I loved sales and the idea that I was in control of my income.

We made our money on commissions. My clients paid me and if I wanted to make more, I would go out and sell more. There was no steady, reliable paycheck. My wife and I had to live far below our means because we never knew when we could lose a large client and our income could drop.

At first, I felt like this was the best path toward financial freedom. But I quickly realized that I was on a treadmill. If I stopped working, my clients stopped paying and my income ended. The harder I worked, the more money I made, but if I stopped working—just like anyone with a normal paycheck—the money stopped coming in. This vehicle would not take me to financial freedom, and I needed to find one that would. Luckily for me, I found that wealth vehicle before I was knocked down. I would never get on the sales treadmill again.

As I lay in my bed, still immobile, I was told that my boss was flying in to visit me. I knew what was coming. It was very considerate of the company I worked for to wait and keep me on the payroll at least until I could talk again. The visit was short and considerate; I knew they would not be able to keep me employed. It had been months, after all, and I still had not left the hospital. It was understood that my employment had ended, and I would not be coming back. We still didn't know when I would leave the hospital or if I would ever walk again. I lay there looking out my window, paralyzed and now unemployed, but not scared and not worried.

CHAPTER 1

How I Found Self Storage and How It Saved Me

I believe that self storage offers more income and wealth creation than any commercial real estate asset, or more than any other commercial real estate asset, on the market. It is through self storage that I was able to become financially free. It was through self storage that I was able to gain enough passive income that when I could no longer work, I didn't need to.

Self storage can provide returns far beyond any other real estate asset class can offer because there are opportunities for leverage in many areas. The industry has come out of obscurity (in terms of its rating in the investment world) and is still somewhat unknown—but that's changing.

GETTING OFF THE TREADMILL

Before I started investing and owned self storage, I started out in the insurance industry, working at a company called Aflac. Yes, the one with the duck.

From there, I worked at a local brokerage firm selling insurance. Later, I moved back to my home city to work with my father, who had a brokerage firm.

Sales allowed me to grow my income. My father taught me about the beauty of a reoccurring, residual sale. We would sell to a client, and every time that client paid for insurance, we got a piece of it. It was a way for those who are hungry and driven to make a lot of money. I was definitely hungry and had a lot of drive and I had the best mentor in the world: my father.

He showed me all the ins and outs of insurance. I got to work with amazing people, and I loved my job. For years, we sold to clients and grew his brokerage firm.

But sales is a very hard thing to scale because it depends on people. It depends on you making that money. Going out, getting the paper signed, servicing the clients, and being available at all times, ready to work.

Ready to pick up the phone when that client calls.

My father used to say 90% of our assets go home at night and it's true. For us and the other sales guys in our Idaho brokerage firm, when we went home, it ended. And if we didn't come back in the morning, no money was made. This statement stuck with me—and it stuck with me for a long time. As I started to try to further grow, I decided it would be easier to buy companies then it would be to sell to an individual employer. Instead, we could buy blocks of businesses, therefore condensing the time of growth. The difficulty with sales and maintaining clients is that you don't own that revenue stream. Clients want to make changes and things happen. They fire you, they leave, and that revenue stream ends. It is extremely unpredictable.

And not secured.

This was extremely frustrating for me. And at one point, although I felt like I was my own boss, I was making good sales money, and I was living the dream—I soon realized that I was on a treadmill.

And every day that I woke up, I had to climb back on that treadmill to make money and if I stopped, I fell off.

I felt stuck. I just wasn't going anywhere. Not that I'm complaining. I was making good money from my sales job. I had a wonderful family. I got to work with my father as my partner, which brought me tremendous joy, but we were still running in place.

I knew we needed to own and control the sources of revenue. Whereas our revenue source was coming from a client—if you are employed, your revenue source may be coming from a boss. The only difference between me and someone who was employed (not on commissions) was that I had lots of bosses instead of one.

In order to not have any bosses, I had to own and control the revenue.

I began to create a path, a system that would take us off the treadmill to financial freedom.

The normal process of this, or as I call it, the *wealth process,* is fairly simple. Make money, save money, invest in your *wealth vehicle,* and scale.

I had been saving and investing, but I hadn't yet found the wealth vehicle that would help me reach my goals.

> **Wealth vehicle:** the business and system you build that takes you to financial freedom.

I wanted to generate income from an investment and preserve that investment value at the same time. I wanted to know I could choose to get off that treadmill without losing my income.

Self storage can produce a known rate of return that does not depend on market appreciation or, to a large extent, whether the economy is moving up or down. It has predictable cash flow with the opportunity to increase it.

MY FIRST PURCHASE

As a way of diversifying out of insurance sales, my father and I bought a small storage facility close to the border of Canada in Idaho. It was at best a fourth-tier market. There was no pavement. It had no office and no toilets.

We were excited about the opportunities it represented because of what we thought was a lack of the right kind of management. But later, we would learn that there could be so much more.

It's funny now because that first facility had some cash flow but never made big money. In fact, we sold it for a little less than we'd bought it for, but we had learned so much and we had found what we thought was a diamond in the rough.

And by a diamond in the rough, I don't mean the storage facility. The diamond is the asset class itself.

We took our capital from that sale and rolled it into another market, into a little larger facility. Within eight months, after turning around that facility, we sold that and bought another one worth over eight times the value of that small facility by the Canadian border.

We did that by putting very little extra money into it.

I had a philosophy, an underlying approach to self storage and the self storage world. It's that self storage is not a real estate asset. It's a business.

SELF STORAGE IS NOT A REAL ESTATE ASSET; IT'S A BUSINESS

Self storage is a business that offers predictable cash flow with significant upside, while still maintaining all the benefits of a real estate asset—depreciation and appreciation. If you want to invest money into something that preserves your investment and also produces income, your options are limited. Investing in most asset classes of rental income-producing real estate takes a lot of capital to generate any significant amount of income.

Self storage is not like other real estate assets: it's really a retail business. To understand the investment opportunity that self storage represents, you need to know some fundamentals about the industry:

1. Who owns self storage facilities and how that creates opportunity for you

2. Who uses self storage facilities (tenants)

3. How tenants want to use self storage

You also need to understand how technology, the internet, and market trends have affected the industry and created more opportunities.

I learned a tremendous amount about how to research the markets, evaluate the revenue potential of an underperforming facility, and how to upgrade the facility, operations, marketing, and revenue in a repeatable system that I tested for myself. I was still on the treadmill (sales), but I had found my wealth vehicle. I felt I was on top of the world.

Little did I know that in the not-too-distant future, I would be kicked off that treadmill through no choice of mine.

HOW WILL YOU SUPPORT YOURSELF WHEN YOUR TREADMILL STOPS?

The treadmill is the income you make by working for it every day—income that's tied to the hours you work. To make more money, you have to work harder or longer. For many people, *when* you get off the treadmill is a retirement question and a personal choice, assuming you will remain able to work until you choose to stop.

With no warning, I experienced a complete collapse of my health and ability to work.

The situation was devastating and terrifying, but I was able to focus on my situation and healing with no worries that my family would be without income to support us. The self storage businesses I had purchased continued to produce passive income, even while I was on life support.

HOW GUILLAIN-BARRÉ STOPPED MY TREADMILL

In the introduction I gave you a glimpse into a day of the living hell that had become my life. Little did I know that my body was being attacked by a deadly foe—myself. My white blood cells had turned against me and started to attack my nervous system.

This happened suddenly, without warning. I was still running several miles a day. I was operating our state's largest brokerage firm, which was a branch of a national company, one of the top three in the industry. I had also created a storage facility company with a $100M in assets.

Things could not be better. It seemed like nothing could go wrong. I loved my job. I loved my wealth vehicle. We had big plans. In fact, we had just had our fourth child.

We had been traveling when I first felt something was off, but I didn't think much of it.

And upon coming home, I knew I was in a lot of pain. I went to the hospital. They sent me home because nothing was wrong with me. But within hours, I was paralyzed.

My wife took me back to the hospital where they argued. What was happening? What was wrong with me? Then, in just a matter of a couple days, I lost my ability to breathe. I was put under and ventilated.

Everything outside looked normal but inside, my body was raging war with itself and before anyone could figure out what was happening, my white blood cells had destroyed my nervous system, so my brain could no longer communicate with my body.

My body was in searing pain, but I was unable to communicate. I was on breathing tubes and feeding tubes, with machines all around me, blinking and making noises, and it felt impossible to sleep because of the pain. It didn't matter what pain meds I was given. Nothing seemed to stop it.

As I looked around, it seemed like every single day, the nightmare was never-ending. In fact, I got worse and worse and worse.

Until finally, I believed that I would never come out of it—that it would be the end. And I hoped that my wife wouldn't leave me for the rest of my life on the tubes.

At this point, I obviously couldn't work. In fact, I didn't even care. I didn't even think about working. I didn't think about my clients nor did I think about my boss or the company that I worked for.

I just focused on not dying.

After months, I was finally able to speak. I was finally able to communicate. Our whole life was uprooted and the future of my life, as well as my family's lives, was unknown.

When I asked if I would ever use my arms or hands again or walk, the doctors couldn't give me an answer. But slowly, I healed and started to come back. After being able to talk, I began to use my arms again and my hands again. I had to relearn how to do everything. I couldn't eat on my own. I couldn't bathe on my own. Nothing. Like a newborn baby, everything was new and everything was a struggle. I had lost over 70 pounds of body weight and muscle mass.

Lucky for me, we did have our newborn baby, Theo, who spent the first part of his life with me in hospitals. My only joy during this time was being able to see my children.

I was sent to a long-term care facility, a location where they put people that needed to be on life support, with no date to leave. I couldn't even remember the last time that I had been out of a hospital, or which hospital I was in.

My nurses were incredible, but one thing was clear: I would not be working anytime soon.

After months of being on life support and in rehabilitation centers, they sent me home. But when I was helped by my family back into the house where we had lived before my collapse, I was not the same person I was the night I had left. I went home in a wheelchair. My brother, Taylor, who was living in Hawaii, moved in with us to take care of me alongside my wife and four children.

I had to have help bathing and I spent my days in bed, still in tremendous pain, hardly able to function for any length of time.

Our family, friends, and church took care of our family during this time. But so did self storage.

Self storage saved my family's financial life. We remained comfortable. We didn't have to leave my house. I was lucky that the home I left was the home I came back to. Our bills were paid. My kids went to school and were able to spend time with their dad.

My wife didn't have to get a job and leave me paralyzed at home. She could tend to me and our children, who were still not sure what was going on—just happy their father was alive.

And as we sat at home caring for my needs and trying to create a new life while I tried to gain strength and learn how to walk again, we collected income. While we tried to put our lives back together again, our storage business kept making money and in fact, it grew in value and revenue.

It would be over two and a half years until I was able to return to work—loaded up on medication and with my legs in braces, but at least I could finally walk again.

Not only did self-storage save my financial life, but it created a tremendous amount of wealth. And it did so in a time frame that I didn't know was possible.

So, how did I get to this point? How did I create millions and millions in value and become financially free through this obscure asset class?

Next, I'll show you how to create a wealth vehicle from self storage.

WHY SELF STORAGE?

Self storage is the newest real estate asset class, and it has gone from junkyard to upscale neighborhood status, and from chain-link fencing to climate-controlled options with meeting rooms, over the past 10 to 15 years. It is a growing $40-60 billion industry.

The self storage industry is currently in a consolidation phase, coming from a historically fragmented ownership. Buying from individuals presents unique opportunities for several reasons. At the same time, property management companies exist now that will manage a facility for you, if you don't want to be involved.

You can also set up your own management with employees and systems to essentially run themselves. This can make it a truly passive investment and offers the greatest leveraging opportunities.

Self storage has also been under the radar because banks didn't have a performance model and therefore wouldn't finance them. After self storage revenue posted strong performance through the Great Recession, these businesses started getting attention. Investors started realizing self storage revenues are recession-resilient.

Banks had another reason for avoiding self-storage: they wanted to fund an investment, not a business—something that had to be operated. Once companies offering third-party management that specialized in self storage became available, the asset class was much more attractive to institutional buyers. They could buy it and hire a company to run it, so it was a completely hands-off investment. Banks that used to be reluctant to fund them now want to fund them.

WHAT MAKES SELF STORAGE RECESSION-RESILIENT?

To understand why self storage is recession-resilient, you need to understand why people use self storage. During a recession, people are often forced to downsize, but they don't want to get rid of their stuff so they rent storage units. People who have to move their households use storage units. People who have too much stuff use storage units. People who buy in nice neighborhoods that don't allow RV parking use storage units. People in apartment complexes use storage units. And a recent trend is that people who run online businesses use storage units because there's no room for their inventory in their house. And there's more.

Recent economic trends have favored self storage. Rising real estate costs and lower costs of consumption allow us to have more things but less space to store those things. According to the National Association of Home Builders, the average size of a new, single-family home dropped from 2,700 feet in 2015, to under 2,600 in 2018.

Also, the cost of traveling has decreased and people are more mobile. They're more willing to get up and move. House rentals have been trending upward in the United States, meaning more people are choosing to rent than own their own home—this trend also benefits self storage.

Outside of economic trends, one of the greatest opportunities for any commercial real estate investor lies in how the industry is made up. In self-storage, 80% of self storage owners in the industry are single operators, or what are called "mom and pop" facilities. This is the reverse of what you find in other asset classes like commercial and apartments, where the vast majority is owned by institutional investors. Now, in self storage this is beginning to change. The self-storage world is consolidating, but that is where the advantage lies. An individual can be a part of the consolidation and has more opportunities to buy self storage facilities and not be in competition with institutional buyers than any other commercial asset class.

In addition to consolidation, the way self storage facilities are run has undergone tremendous change, largely due to technology advancements and the internet. Because so many facilities are individually owned, their use of technology varies widely. Property management systems software (PMS) plus automation of everything from opening the gate to signing contracts has streamlined many operations that used to be manual. You can buy a self storage facility that has not kept up with the changes and turn it around for relatively little capital expenditure. This creates tremendous opportunity for operations improvement and expense reduction.

A VALUE-ADD STRATEGY

I learned how to identify undervalued locations, purchase them, and implement process and capital improvements that multiplied not only the value of the property but also dramatically increased the revenue in a very short period of time—consistently in under a year. This forced appreciation allowed me to either collect revenue for investing, refinance after revenue and valuation have stabilized to obtain the cash to go do it again—my approach has generally been to either collect revenue for new investments or sell to buy up, and not to refinance in less than three to five years. Since I sold that first northern Idaho location, this has been a very successful strategy. I have built a portfolio of self storage businesses to a value of $100M-plus.

What I want to show you is how you can do this for yourself—how you can find underperforming facilities in great markets and turn them around.

There are self storage facilities of all sizes and costs in all markets. There are small storage facilities that sell for under $1M. And then there are massive facilities in first-tier markets that sell for over $20M (more on markets later).

In self storage, you can start small in good markets, create value, increase income, and use that increase in value and income to buy more facilities and keep growing.

Chapter 2 describes the self storage industry and why it's a good investment. Chapter 3 explains the different ways you can enter the industry—buy, build, or convert. Chapter 4 explains how to understand self storage markets (supply and demand), identify a market where you can compete, and how to find deals. Chapter 5 is about how to finance a self storage project and work with brokers and banks. Chapter 6 is about evaluating self storage facilities, the competition, and the deal. You need to read chapters 4, 5, and 6 before you are ready to go shopping. Chapter 7 explains what's involved in running your new facility, chapter 8 is about how to reduce risk, and chapter 9 is about next steps to reach your investment goals.

THE PLAYBOOK IN A NUTSHELL

Before we dive into everything, I want you to have the big picture on the process. This playbook is based on my own version of the self storage wealth vehicle: purchase an existing facility with the right characteristics for leveraging a value-add strategy.

While purchasing an existing facility is only one of the three ways you can enter the industry, it offers more leveraging opportunities with less risk than the other two, and it's a great way to learn as you go. You can buy it, learn the industry by improving and growing the performance of that first purchase, and take revenue or refinanced cash out to invest in another while continuing to collect the revenue from the first. Buying a second location may be optional for you, depending on your goals. Many people buy one facility and find that it helps them meet their goals. Others have gone on to create their own self storage empires as I have.

The process is scalable both up and down; you can start bigger or smaller to fit your goals.

Here is my successful playbook for leveraging your capital through self storage.

THE PLAYBOOK

1. Identify Your Goals and Resources
Knowing your investment goals, the amount of capital you have (or want to have) to invest, and how you intend to manage your first location will help you choose the right way for you to enter the industry. See chapter 3.

2. Identify a Market and a Facility and Find the Deal
Identify a market by evaluating recent and projected growth of population and employers in an area. Research all the self storage facilities in a selected area. Data aggregation software can help with this but nothing is foolproof. You still need to drive around and find all the self storage facilities. Look at all the facilities and evaluate their operations to find the underperformers. See chapters 4 and 6.

3. Perform Due Diligence
Verify the market you've chosen is the right one by researching the locale using a combination of online searches, data aggregation software, and feet-on-the-ground research. This will include secret shopping and reaching out to city planning and zoning organizations. See chapters 4 and 6.

4. Save or Raise Money

While you may think you need to have the money before you go shopping, the truth is no bank will talk to you until you've identified the facility you want to buy. They need to know the specifics in order to underwrite it. Determine how much capital you need for a down payment to get started in the self storage industry and then work toward obtaining it. At the same time, work on how to obtain financing for the rest of the purchase. See chapter 5.

5. Purchase Your Facility

Negotiate price and financing and purchase your facility. Your market research will equip you to know what price you can pay. Focus on revenue potential and upside—what I call "money on the table." Calculate your own projections for future revenue and value. This will be covered in chapter 6.

6. Create Value Through Improvements and Targeted Marketing

Improve the facility to attract the right customer and to meet the demand for the kind of storage services you've identified in the area. Upgrade the technology to streamline daily operations. Set policies to protect your revenue stream and maximize the length of stay for your tenants. Build your team with directly hired staff or third-party management, plus legal, insurance, and most importantly, marketing. See chapter 7.

7. Build Capital by Collecting Revenue or Refinancing

Whether you should collect investment capital for your next investment goal through the revenue from your first facility or by refinancing or obtaining a line of credit to take advantage of the value you've created depends on the local market, the economy in general, and your specific circumstances. I'll explain how to evaluate this. See chapters 8 and 9.

You also have the option of simply selling the facility for what it is worth with your improvements. You lose the revenue from that facility, but you can grow your capital and invest in other opportunities with it. If you find you've made a mistake in your choice and it's not going to help you meet your goals, this is the thing to do and was the reason we sold our first one. It was our elementary school education in self storage and what we got from it was knowledge. I'll tell more of that story in the How to Get Started in Self Storage chapter.

Using the information I share in this book plus the online resources you can find at SelfStorageIncome.com, you can use self storage to reach your investment goals, no matter what they are.

KEY TAKEAWAYS

▶ Change your perspective on self storage. View it not as a real estate asset but as a business with a known rate of return.

▶ The key to this is to evaluate your market (go as big as you can but probably not first tier), do your homework on evaluating the purchase and the business, and if it's right for you, buy an existing location for the right price.

▶ Learn how to run it and improve it to 2X (or more) the value, while collecting cash flow.

▶ The magic is that you can 2X the value in less than a year and it doesn't depend on the real estate market. You are not depending on appreciation for your return.

CHAPTER 2

Overview of the Self Storage Industry and Why It's a Great Investment Opportunity

The primary purpose of self storage is to secure people's belongings. To really understand the industry, you need to understand what self storage is, who uses it and why, and what types of self storage facilities are available, plus the trends in the marketplace.

WHAT IS SELF STORAGE?

People need a place to store their stuff, and they want it close to their home or business. Self storage provides a unit they can access any time of day or night, usually through a secure, gated entrance. You provide that place with a lease agreement that is month to month. You provide an office where people can come in to see if your facility is where they want to keep their stuff. So it has a daily operations component that no other real estate asset requires.

The worst thing about self storage is also the best thing about self storage.

The worst thing is it's a business—it's operations-heavy. You have customers coming in and out. The best thing is if you can find a self storage facility that is mismanaged, you can dramatically increase its revenue by improving the operations and implementing effective marketing.

You have offerings for the customers—not only different-sized units but multiple lines of products to sell them. This includes renters insurance, pallets, boxes, and wrap. You can also offer lighting, climate control, and power. That means you can offer units for wine storage, vehicle storage, and pharmaceutical storage. You can cater to businesses that need to store inventory, internet companies that are running entirely from a storage unit, and just normal people moving.

People rent space from you, but they don't have the same rights as a tenant in an apartment building. A self storage owner has the right to evict for any reason—failure to pay, violation of a policy, etc. You're not putting anyone on the street if you evict.

Self storage markets are extremely localized. In general, people don't want to use one that's more than five miles from their home.

Self storage revenue management has a sales component you don't find in other real estate assets. As an investment, an apartment building is an apartment building—you don't have these options. You rent all the units and walk away. With self storage, you have a showroom. So when people walk in, it looks really nice and you can upsell them.

You may think that seems like a lot of work. Yes—and you hire people and train them to do that work, and that's where the upside comes. You can improve those operations and maximize the revenue. Once you put systems in place, you can walk away.

The short time frame of the lease in self storage represents both a risk and an opportunity. Customers can leave tomorrow, and you can raise the rents monthly.

HOW TO LOOK AT SELF STORAGE MARKETS

Self storage markets are approximately defined by the population base around them. Large metropolitan areas are *first-tier* markets—think New York, Houston, Miami, LA, Seattle, Chicago. These markets are dominated by REIT (real estate investment trust) ownership, which are large institutional players. Facilities in these markets usually demand higher purchase prices and higher barriers of entry to get into that market. If you are starting out with your first storage facility in a first-tier market, you need to do a lot of research, collect a lot of data, and proceed very carefully.

Second-tier markets are smaller cities but still can have larger metropolitan areas—think Portland, Oregon; Austin, Texas; and Nashville, Tennessee. These are large cities and large metropolitan areas, but do not reach the size and scale of first-tier markets.

Third-tier markets are outside metropolitan areas, so they have a good population base. They have commerce and normal amenities, but they are generally overlooked. Albuquerque, New Mexico, and Oklahoma City are probably third-tier markets, along with Spokane, Washington; Boise, Idaho; and Omaha, Nebraska.

Fourth-tier markets are small cities with no large airport and not a lot of infrastructure.

Fifth-tier markets are small hometowns.

For the purposes of this book, this is how I generally classify markets. Many people see these markets differently and will have different guidelines for what makes a second-tier or first-tier market. Because customers of self storage tend to choose facilities very close to their home or business, the area that defines the "market" for any given facility is about a three- to five-mile radius around that facility. This creates opportunity because if you find an area is oversupplied, drive a few miles and check again. Things could be very different, even within small cities.

There's more to evaluating a market than just its size. Especially in the smaller markets, whether there's growth or stagnation is critical to determine before you decide there's potential. Stagnation is bad for self storage business; movement of people and goods benefits the self storage industry.

WHO USES SELF STORAGE?

The who (who uses self storage) and why they use it has been changing too, and this is part of understanding the industry. In general, approximately 10% of the population uses self storage.

Whether a self storage facility is surrounded by subdivisions or dominated by business parks affects the kind of customers who will use that facility, and you need to understand the needs of those customers to attract them.

Understanding the customer (tenant) is a critical part of finding investment opportunities in self storage. Storage customers are all looking for different things. They have different needs and wants but they generally fall into three categories, based on what is most important to them:

1. Price
2. Convenience
3. Quality

These priorities also dictate how much they will pay per square foot (SF) for storage space. A run-down facility with little security and no curb appeal will attract price-conscious tenants. These tenants might be paying $0.30 to $0.50 per square foot. Part of the leverage opportunity in self storage is to renovate that facility, upgrade the operations and customer service, and market to the quality-conscious tenants who are willing to pay up to $0.80 per square foot (and that's a ballpark; some of our facilities charge more than that). Do the math—the revenue upside is large.

The key to the value-add strategy for investing in self storage by purchasing existing facilities is to identify facilities occupied by price-conscious tenants and upgrade the facility to attract tenants who will pay a higher price. More customized offerings and add-on products can also create more value. The revenue increase can be dramatic, once you implement these things.

The quality-conscious customers who will pay a higher price are typically homeowners with children, and usually it's the adult female in the household who makes the decision to choose a self storage facility. So if your facility doesn't appeal to that demographic, you are not attracting quality-conscious customers. That means the facility needs to look nice, be clean, well-lit and well maintained, and feel safe and secure.

Businesses are increasingly using self storage and you can customize your offerings to attract them, including adding meeting spaces and office space for lease. Lighting and power inside units can allow small businesses to operate entirely out of a storage unit.

TYPES OF SELF STORAGE
SIZE

Self storage facilities are typically classified first by size as small, medium, or large.

Small facilities operationally speaking, have to control cost carefully because the cost will eat up your margin quickly.

I've included ballpark square footage ranges so you can see how they break down:

- Small: 10,000-50,000 SF
- Medium: 50,000-100,000 SF
- Large: 100,000-plus SF

An example of a small self storage facility. This one had no office or showroom and five buildings like the ones shown.

An example of a medium self storage facility, between 50K and 100K SF.

An example of a large self storage facility, more than 100K SF.

As an investment, each size has pros and cons.

In addition to size, you can classify self storage by what they are designed to store. For example, you can have climate-controlled, outdoor, drive-up, parking, and specialized storage such as for documents or wine. Many facilities will have a combination of offering types and for the purposes of this discussion, we'll focus on size. The reason we focus on size is because this has so much to do with the cost and operations.

It's important to understand how revenue and expenses work for each size. For example, many of the expenses in a 30-40K SF facility exist in an 80K SF facility. The main difference is in the margin. But when looking at where you want to start and what you want to invest in, you may be constrained by capital.

When I got started, we started in smaller facilities with the capital we had. When we could, we moved up to medium and then to large. At the time of this writing, it's my belief that smaller facilities must include many different strategies, including call centers and online access, to replace the expense of on-site management. This can be done through technology which we will address. The cost of a manager in a small facility can often decimate any profit. I would encourage you to automate or use it as a starting point to move up.

Facilities of 50-100K SF were where we had our bread and butter—medium-sized facilities on average around 85K SF. We built our portfolio mainly with these.

Large facilities, 100K SF plus, have their place but you need to be careful. In my hometown, many people build 200K SF facilities. These are behemoths that I think are a poor use of capital. Here's why: in low density areas, large outdoor facilities over 200K SF can dramatically increase the cost for acquisition of storage facilities as well as dilute the need for storage in a three-mile radius. In many locations, there isn't enough demand to support that much square footage at the price per SF you are looking for. We have seen that in our area, where people build 150K SF facilities and then have trouble meeting their revenue per SF targets. This is poorly executed planning.

The reason people will sometimes do this is because they think that after a certain point in expenses, the more SF the better. I know people who own very large facilities, but they built them on land that was purchased over 30 years ago so their cost of entry is extremely low. Then it's advantageous to build more because of the low cost. But in general, at over 150K SF, you must be extremely careful with the execution so you don't flood the three-mile radius with more SF than is demanded.

I suggest focusing on medium facilities. I do own some from 100K to 150K SF and they can be great investments and great opportunities, but you need to be more careful and focus on supply and demand.

The size also affects the management. We have extremely large indoor facilities at over 100K SF with everything from drive-up, RV park, dump, indoor units, and indoor drive-up units with technology. And with many gates and doors, all entrances and exits have to be considered. How the consumer utilizes larger facilities will change how you manage them, because often you need more resources. In good markets you'll get more revenue, so that shouldn't be a problem.

For medium facilities, you have the best of both worlds: a manager on-site combined with technology and automation that makes you competitive in the marketplace, and you can get a higher revenue per SF while still being able to offer everything your customers need.

Choosing which type will work best for you is important and typically starts with the answers to two questions:

1. How much money do you have to invest (and how will you finance the rest)?
2. How will you operate it: manage it yourself or hire a management company?

How much capital you need depends on the market quality and size of facility you are buying. Financing the rest can be done in a variety of ways, and more on that will be covered in the chapter on financing. Individually owned facilities can sometimes be purchased with seller financing, which can be a powerful leveraging tool.

PERCEIVED VALUE AND CURB APPEAL

The perceived value of a facility is tied directly to the type of tenant they attract. The way the facility looks and feels will appeal to your customers in terms of price, convenience, or quality.

- Price sensitive people: Just as you would expect. Minimal curb appeal, basic offerings. Just a place to put your stuff. Location is not important. Security is not important and there may or may not be staff—if there are staff, most of the time they are not well trained.
- People who want convenience: This is the drive-by place with not much going for it except it's on the way home. It will usually match the look of the nearby subdivision because city planning departments require it.
- People who expect quality: This is the high-end place that stands out. It has a high-end look, top security, well-trained staff, and is offering ancillary products and services besides just renting a unit. And it has to have a good location.

Location is a primary consideration when you are looking for an investment.

> # You can't change the location of a self storage facility, so evaluate that before anything else.

You can't change the location, so that needs to be right from the beginning. You can change the rest of its physical characteristics.

WHAT MAKES THE BEST INVESTMENT OPPORTUNITY?

If you decide the way you want to enter the self storage industry is by purchasing an existing facility, the key is to find one that is currently undervalued because it has one or more of these characteristics:

- Needs updating and upgrading
- Has little or no online presence
- Has little or no curb appeal
- Isn't being managed or marketed effectively

If you can find a facility for sale with all of those characteristics, it's a true goldmine (in a good market). But having just one of those characteristics can be enough for a great leveraging opportunity. This is the essence of my value-add strategy.

HOW KNOWLEDGE CAN REDUCE RISK

The value-add system that my partners and I work off of has worked on over 1M SF of self storage that we currently own. This system is repeatable and once you've done it the first time, you can utilize the same systems on each subsequent investment. I have gone on to build self storage from the ground up and also convert existing buildings into self storage that are now successful revenue-producing assets. I have personally experienced all facets of self storage I will tell you about in this book.

Here's an example: With a 60,000 SF facility, the revenue generated per SF per month in a traditional second-tier market is, let's say, $0.50. This is $30K/month or $360K per year. You may have a 38% expense ratio on that investment: management, technology, and capital expenditures. In general, the expense ratio will average 35-42%—snow removal, etc. It's rarely under 35% or over 45%.

That means you net $223,200 with 10% vacancy. At 7% cap rate, that costs you $2.8M. That's a standard real estate calculation. That 7% cap rate isn't anything to be proud of (this is before you pay any debt).

It's not the 7 cap that matters. Self storage has a value creation mechanism that other real estate assets don't have. We spruce up the office of the facility with a capital expenditure of $50-$100K, and we can turn that facility around very quickly. What we're looking for is to take that $0.50 per SF up to $0.80 per SF. Find a poor operator, do basic improvements, and you can do this. And this is on the low end for an improvement differential.

At $0.65 per SF per month, the gross revenue would be $468K per year ($0.65 x 60,000 SF = $39,000 x 12 months). The net on this property would now be $331,200. At a 7 cap, that facility is now valued at $4,731,428. That means you're going to make $1,931,428 ($4,731,428 − $2,800,000) on that facility.

The increase in value and revenue can happen in a very short time frame—under a year, in most cases. And because it is a business, you have an asset that's valued higher than when you bought it, and it produces more revenue, if you made the right improvements and market it correctly.

What I'm saying is that, while buying with debt can be a risk, if you educate yourself on the industry and know the facility you are buying is underperforming and you can double the revenue per square foot that it produces, it's less of a risk. It's an *informed risk*—and you are investing in the *revenue potential* of the property that you know how to produce.

SELF STORAGE IS A REVENUE-PRODUCING ASSET

Self storage is a real estate asset that produces rental income but in reality, it is a business. All businesses produce revenue—how much they produce depends on how the business is managed. A mismanaged business will not produce the revenue it is capable of, and in the self storage industry, this commonsense statement highlights the tremendous investment opportunities that are available if you know how to leverage them.

Several other aspects of the industry and characteristics of how self storage facilities are operated make it a unique investment opportunity with growth potential unmatched in any other real estate asset class. It offers opportunities for multiple people with multiple goals and outlooks, in every part of the U.S. and Canada.

As with many other sectors of the commercial real estate world, self storage investors are embracing new trends to improve efficiencies, make the tenant experience better, and create value wherever they can. Electronic access control is becoming common, with keycard, biometric, and phone/app-based access to the facility. Specialized climate-controlled facilities are gaining momentum and are particularly popular with auto/boat/collectible enthusiasts who rent the units for their collections.

Data analytics are also driving changes in the self storage market. Collecting customer data to better serve their needs, marketing via the web, and digitizing reservation and payment systems are all becoming standard in many major self storage markets. Many owner-investors have also started offering advanced security systems that give tenants the ability to watch over their units via webcam. Tech is disrupting every industry, and the self storage sector is not immune to these changes.

A self storage business is more like retail than real estate. There are lots of offerings, and customer service is a critical aspect of the operation. Facilities can provide other services like meeting spaces and more. This is part of the change that's happening—but more on that later.

Unlike an apartment building, you can give a self storage facility a complete facelift and remodel without major work and capital expenditure. It's relatively simple and fast. This is a big part of the value-add strategy, and it's why you want to look for facilities in need of upgrading to buy.

If you can improve operations and systems, build a management team who understands your customers, and upgrade your marketing to target the higher-paying customers, you can put everything in place, start collecting cash flow, and walk away to start over with a new facility.

OFFERINGS

The products you offer can differentiate you from the competition. Know what size of units and what additional amenities your tenants want, and you will be able to charge top rates and maintain a high occupancy.

Self storage can protect and safeguard belongings in several different ways:
- Protected from the weather:
    · Covered
    · Enclosed
- Secured with gated access, cameras, and locks
- Specialized storage:
    · Climate controlled for wine, pharmaceuticals, etc.
    · Power for trickle charges for classic cars and other motorized vehicles
    · Interior lighting for inventory and business operations storage
- Included related services:
    · RV dumps
    · Wi-Fi
    · Meeting rooms
    · Tenant insurance

Changing the offerings can be a leveraging opportunity too, so keep an eye out for that when you are evaluating a facility. We found and purchased a large facility that was not well occupied. At first, this can be a bad sign but upon further investigation, we noticed that the facility had five buildings, all with 5 x 5 units. Literally hundreds and hundreds of 5 x 5 units. It was built this way because the developer wanted to maximize his price per square foot.

But there wasn't demand for hundreds and hundreds of 5 x 5s. So we bought the facility and removed walls and made 10 x 10s as well as other sizes within those buildings, and they filled up rapidly. We were able to change the product offering to match market needs.

MARKETS

We've defined markets by the size of the city they're in. In addition to understanding the size of the city and its economic indicators, what makes a market a "good" or "bad" one is the supply and demand in that market—and we're talking in a three- to five-mile radius.

Any size market can be a bad one if it's overbuilt, so determining the supply and demand climate in any area is critical to your buy or don't buy (or build or don't build, or convert) decision. Researching good markets has more to do with identifying competitors in the area than how many customers are nearby. How many SF of storage per capita is in that area? And a key part of this is identifying the strengths and weaknesses of the competitors in that market. I'll mention this again, but when you see the underperforming competitors at capacity with a waiting list, you know there's good demand and not enough supply.

I would rather go to a third-tier market that has a lot of demand and not a lot of people building new facilities than a second-tier market that's overbuilt.

LEARN TO IDENTIFY OVERBUILT MARKETS

Any market that is overbuilt is not a good place to start, no matter what size it is. Research the local market for competitors in the area and availability of sites with the right zoning where new ones could be built. Also build a safety margin into your valuation of any potential purchase and don't leverage so much that if your revenue dropped by 10-20%, you couldn't make the payments. For more on how to evaluate markets, see the chapter on valuation.

HOW THE SELF STORAGE INDUSTRY HAS CHANGED

Self storage has gained a reputation for consistent revenue with high returns. It has also gained one of being recession resistant.

Historically, self storage originated in junkyards and industrial parks. As a real estate asset class, they are operations-heavy and as a result, banks typically have not viewed them as lend-worthy. The industry has changed to basically mirror hotels, and now is considered like a class A real estate asset. Instead of being located in junkyards and industrial parks, they are in your neighborhood—every neighborhood. And cities demand that they look nice.

Compared to apartment buildings, self storage ownership is fragmented—meaning about 70% of them are owned by individuals. I call this "mom and pop" ownership. Only 30% are owned by institutional investors. This is essentially the reverse of apartment building ownership, where 80% is institutionally owned and 20% is individually owned.

In the last 10 years, third-party property management services that specialize in self storage have become available. This has changed the investment potential dramatically, and the self storage market is in a consolidation phase as a result. Even though institutional investors have started to invest in self storage, it's still an opportunity for individual investors, with many localized markets left to find.

Historically, banks have not viewed self storage facilities as an investment opportunity and therefore financing to purchase these facilities has been difficult to find. During the Great Recession, self storage revenue performance was tested, and showed that these businesses could maintain revenue better than almost any other real estate asset. Banks have started viewing these businesses differently and are more willing to finance them.

Another change happened in terms of how consumers viewed these businesses. A TV show that came on the air just before the recession showcased huge, beautiful facilities in southern California and became popular. As a result, consumers became more aware of and more familiar with these facilities and changed their expectations (they were not viewed as junkyards anymore). Now, many self storage facilities look more like hotels than storage facilities.

TECHNOLOGY

Technology for operations and marketing is a huge aspect of the self storage industry. We get 80% of our tenants online. We were buying facilities five years ago that didn't even have a website.

No longer do people choose where to store their stuff by seeing the sign on the street. They search online and make the choice about which one to visit based on the website experience—from their mobile device. So the first step in market research is to do your own online searches as if you were a customer. Technology changes have happened so rapidly that many individual owners have not kept up with those changes, and that's part of the opportunity. A facility with a poor or nonexistent website represents a golden opportunity for an investor and a turnoff for the customer.

Technology streamlines operations and can save significantly on operating expenses. The first step here is to choose a PMS (property management system) that has on open interface (this allows a marketing partner to share data) and connects all aspects of the operations, from signing the contract to online and automated payments, buying insurance, renewals, and gate access. New ones are hitting the market, like Tenant Inc. with their Hummingbird platform, that will change the way people use and think about these property management systems.

Sophisticated security systems are another aspect of technology in the industry. Cameras that record comings and goings and what is brought in and removed from every unit on the premise protect the self storage facility and the tenants.

How you conduct market research has also benefited from technology advances. Data aggregation companies that specialize in self storage offer services to assist you in evaluating potential markets. These services are exceptionally valuable because of the fragmented ownership in this industry.

More details on implementing technology in self storage operations are covered in the valuation and operation chapters.

MACROECONOMICS

There are recent economic forces that have helped the self storage industry, including rising costs of building (of homes) and changes in homeownership. On the political front, many cities are becoming more and more stringent about what they allow you to have on your property. At the same time, the cost of toys and consumer items has decreased. All of these macroeconomic trends are helping self storage markets to flourish.

What makes an investment opportunity is usually a combination of factors. You can't ignore trends in consumer spending, cost of living, and consumer financial products when you evaluate an opportunity. In the self storage industry, these things are driving demand. I've already mentioned how fragmented ownership is in the self storage industry—that is, more facilities are owned by individuals than by institutions—and the recent increase in availability of third-party management services to run these businesses.

These and other trends are contributing to what I think of as the "perfect storm" in self storage.

Housing Trends and Housing Regulations

Residential housing costs are increasing in cost per SF. This has resulted in more people renting and more people downsizing. Homeowners associations are creating stricter regulations around what can be parked on a subdivision lot in terms of recreational vehicles and trailers, and also what can be parked on the street. The cost of rentals has increased also, again leading people to rent smaller units than they did before. As a result, people have less space to store their possessions—both large toys and smaller items like collections.

Consumer Goods Costs and Internet Availability

Manufacturing automation and international competition has driven prices down for many consumer goods. This is happening for several reasons:
- Overseas development through cheap labor
- Mass distribution capabilities and our ability to find anything we want and have it shipped directly to our doors

People buy more stuff because they can afford to. It's also easier than ever before to buy stuff online. The selection of available items in almost every category is growing, and purchasing convenience is growing too. Free two-day shipping allows people to sit at home and purchase with a click.

Financing for Consumer Goods

It is easier than ever to obtain financing for larger recreational items like boats, RVs, dirt bikes, and ATVs and smaller consumer items like furniture, clothing, and appliances. In the 70s, if you didn't have the cash, you didn't buy it. With credit cards and easy-to-obtain financing, needing cash in your pocket in order to buy something is a thing of the past.

The Internet Market

People can sell items online easier than ever before, both used and new. Small online businesses are booming, and owners of those businesses need a space to store their inventory. People are running businesses out of storage units. Also, with the number of brick-and-mortar retail locations for larger businesses shrinking, those businesses are using storage units as part of their supply chain model to solve the "last mile problem" of speedy delivery to the doorstep.

LEVERAGE POTENTIAL IN SELF STORAGE

Self storage provides a unique opportunity to leverage not just your capital but almost *everything:* you leverage your capital; technology in terms of operations, revenue management, and marketing; local laws; and the currently fragmented ownership in this asset class. Because self storage is essentially a retail business, part of your upside is the add-on products you can sell. Those extra lines of products (insurance, packing supplies, etc.) could be anywhere from 5 to 10% of gross revenue. That can translate to millions of dollars. That doesn't happen when you buy an apartment building.

After you've done this once, you also leverage your knowledge and the systems you've already set up to do it again. Now you have everything down and can simply repeat.

MANAGEMENT

The most powerful form of leverage in self storage is the knowledge of how to run one and how to identify one that's being run poorly, leaving money on the table for you to collect.

Many individuals who own self storage don't know how to effectively manage their tenants or their revenue streams with add-on products and services to maximize the profitability of the business. Learn to recognize underperforming locations and evaluate local market demand, and you can capitalize on both the reduced valuation for that asset (to buy at a discount) and your knowledge of how to improve the facility and its operation, to dramatically increase both the revenue and the valuation of the business in a very short period of time.

TECHNOLOGY

Technology advances are one of the biggest changes that has affected the self storage industry. Consumer handheld devices, security networks, and automation of everything from opening security gates, maintaining online inventories, signing contracts, and collecting payments to targeted, localized advertising has changed the self storage industry and the way operations are performed.

A website that's more than a landing page is just the beginning. It is almost guaranteed that an underperforming self storage facility is not utilizing technology at all, or as well as their competitors, and this huge variability in how they are run creates one of the greatest leveraging opportunities in this industry.

When you are researching a market and looking for a location with investment potential, checking their online presence and visibility is one of the first things you should do.

Using technology, you can leverage the underperforming, lower-priced facility by spending a little to upgrade it, implement modern systems, and turn it into a higher quality facility with higher revenues. This can leverage your cap rate—it could double in a year, as we have done multiple times. A higher valuation allows you to refinance, if the revenue has stabilized, and recover your initial capital and then some—while you keep the property and the income it generates.

Automation technology is enabling self storage facilities that don't need an on-site person at all or lower the hours needed to run it. I'll describe more about our first conversion of a Super Kmart that was fully automated, although we still have employees at this location, later in the book. This changes your expense ratio, sometimes dramatically, and can be used to varying degrees, depending on what you want.

YOUR STRATEGY AND KNOWLEDGE

After you've learned from the first self storage facility you own, how to improve operations and profitability, you can leverage the strategy you developed to repeat the process. The knowledge you'll have will make it easier to evaluate the next one you buy, if you are going that route—you'll be able to tell which facilities have greater leverage potential just by looking at them. A facility that's a little older, filled with mostly price-conscious tenants, and operated with low-tech systems has huge potential—if it's in the right market. So you have to do your due diligence in every case. I'll explain that in the chapter on valuation.

Part of your strategy and process is your network of connections, vendors, and your team. Once you have developed those connections, you can use them over and over to buy and upgrade another facility. You don't have to know how to do everything—you need to find others who can help you.

CAPITAL

Self storage is my wealth vehicle of choice for growing capital. Invest, upgrade the facility, market to the right customers, and collect the dramatically increased revenue and benefit from the improved valuation. Collect the revenue or refinance to get your capital back, and do it again—while you continue collecting revenue from the first purchase.

You can buy a self storage facility from an individual if they are open to owner financing. That's another form of leveraging your capital—creative financing with no middleman who charges closing costs and with better terms.

THE DOWNSIDES OF SELF STORAGE INVESTING

Is self storage a safer investment than apartment buildings, retail buildings, or other real estate types? That depends on the opportunities and the markets where those assets exist. What makes an asset safe is how secure the revenues are. Self storage revenues are diverse but it's month to month. You can have more fluctuation in occupancy than other rentals. Apartments have longer term leases.

That short-term occupancy in self storage is also an upside. You can double the rent and see the impact to your bottom line in a short period of time.

Self storage businesses are subject to overbuilt markets, which can make the difference between being profitable and losing money. Another way of saying this is self storage owners are the biggest threat to self storage (competition and not doing adequate research before committing to a new facility).

Because the market is fragmented (owned by Mom and Pop), you can't research it easily. Due diligence looks different and involves more creative approaches, in order to get a true picture of the local market.

Like many other industries, self storage is vulnerable to disruptive technologies and business models, like Airbnb did to the hotel industry—however, Airbnb didn't kill the hotel industry, it just changed it. Who knows when the next Uber for self storage will come along and dramatically change the industry? Some disruptive business models already exist in the self storage space— Clutter and Closetbox (on-demand storage). These services deliver and pick up your items via an app on your phone, as well as store them. These are more common in large cities with extremely high real estate prices; people don't have room to store all their clothes in their apartment, so they store them and have them delivered when they need them.

THE FUTURE OF SELF STORAGE

Businesses are using self storage for everything from storing inventory temporarily for local deliveries to primary storage to run a business. They inspect, fulfill, and do many other business operations out of self storage units. Some units offer lighting and climate control, making them not much different from an office space. Some of our self storage facilities offer not only meeting spaces for businesses to use but also office spaces. So this has already happened in some locations, and is likely to grow.

One of the possible next steps is accepting deliveries of inventory for businesses—and this is sort of the great frontier. As of now, there are laws that prevent accepting deliveries—of course, this varies by state. Some self storage facilities have added P.O. boxes and give certain third-party vendors access to their units.

Right now, you can add a second person onto a unit as a verified person to get in, but you don't want people bringing stuff in, handing it to your manager and saying, oh, this is for Bob. Because the moment you take it on, you take on liability.

The top people in the industry are all trying to figure this out because if you can figure out how to accept without taking legal responsibility—and we think we're really close with what we're doing in automation—that could be a huge industry. You could fill up your facility with just those people. You could charge huge amounts.

KEY TAKEAWAYS

▶ Self storage is a real estate asset that you evaluate like a business, in terms of its revenue potential.

▶ The self storage industry is in a phase of growth and consolidation that still has tremendous investment opportunities.

▶ The historically fragmented nature of the industry is an opportunity to buy from individuals instead of institutions.

▶ The key is finding the ones who haven't caught up with technology yet and capitalizing on that opportunity to buy at an undervalued price. Then, upgrade it with technology, quality-targeted marketing, and a facelift.

CHAPTER 3

How to Get Started in Self Storage

As I look back, a lot of my assumptions about self storage were wrong when I was starting out. We didn't understand things fully or see the big picture. We learned as we went. But the one thing that we did get right was *we got started*. Our overall philosophy was correct, but our execution changed as we came to better understand the industry—the more people we interacted with, the more knowledge we gained, and the more help we received.

There are a hundred reasons to never get started, with new ones coming along all the time. But as I sat paralyzed in the hospital, I knew that one of the greatest decisions I had made in my life—and the lives of my family—was investing in self storage. That decision allowed me to deal with my health collapse without the worry that we would lose our house and my income.

There are three ways you can enter the self storage industry as an investor.

1. Buy an existing facility.
2. Build a new one from the ground up.
3. Convert an existing building into self storage.

My preferable method is to buy underperforming facilities and turn them around. I buy an existing facility with tenants, so it starts paying me from day one, and I have a plan and a path to get to a certain valuation and income level that is known in the marketplace.

This is my preferred method because I can accurately measure the upside—which reduces my risk. I can buy a facility that has an average revenue per SF per month of 50 cents and I can see that my competitors have an average revenue per SF per month of 80 cents. So I know if I can improve the facility, I can reach that point because there is currently demand for it. Yet while I'm turning the facility around and allocating capital and changing the underlying value proposition of that facility to its customers, I'll be getting paid in the process.

Also, it is not unknown to me—my knowledge of the market with the existing facility I just acquired already in that market has less risk because I am not changing the supply.

Knowledge reduces risk.

When you build a self storage facility from the ground up, you take on more risk because you are hoping the demand to fill up that new facility really exists—because you added to the local supply and the demand for that additional supply is unknown.

Not that I don't build and not that I don't like building. Building is a key part of our strategy. Building can be a fantastic way to generate tons of wealth and my partners and I are currently working on potential development projects across the United States. But developing storage facilities adds more risk because of the time it takes to fill them up. If you're comfortable with that, it can be a great way to enter those markets and create wealth.

Converting also works very well. Converting a facility can be a great way to enter into markets and locations that you previously could not have obtained.

Converting a facility adds a whole new level of technicality. When we converted our first facility, we partnered with others who would help us work with the city to obtain the permitting, buy the deal, and convert it into a storage facility with over 100K SF.

We are working on multiple other conversions right now (as of this writing) that have significant upside because cities are so eager for the vacant properties to be used.

There's a lot of future potential with conversions because the retail world is changing—and as the big box stores go away, there's very little use for those buildings in our economy. Self storage tends to be a great answer because if the building has no good use as it sits, prices go down. So you're able to acquire them cheaper than previously, and as they sit vacant, cities want them occupied and are more willing to work with storage developers.

Each of these methods works and can work very well. However, the first route, buying an existing, underperforming facility, offers the greatest leverage opportunities and truly enables all aspects of my value-add strategy. This is how I was able to repeatedly buy underperforming self storage facilities and dramatically increase both the valuation and the revenue of all of them.

My benchmark return for these investments is at least 20% after stabilization. If I can't achieve this, I don't buy it.

Another benefit of the first route, especially for the first-time owner, is that you can learn how to operate one with the first purchase. Choosing a market you can compete in and that you can add value to is important—you need to learn the ins and outs of the business without the brutal competition of the big players.

Once you understand the ins and outs, you can be an informed buyer for additional facilities, and you will know what your expense ratio is for your management methods. That allows you to make informed estimates on the revenue potential of a self storage facility you identify as underperforming. This is the essence of my value-add model for using self storage as a wealth vehicle.

If you have a larger amount of capital to invest, building or converting are viable options. More on that later in this chapter.

Although there are three ways to enter the self storage industry, there are multiple options and you have multiple opportunities in the marketplace—but those opportunities depend on your resources, goals, and needs. Identifying what you have and what you want to achieve is the first step toward getting started in the self storage industry.

AJ'S VALUE-ADD MODEL AND WHY IT WORKS

For the first-time investor and for anyone who wants to build an empire through purchasing and improving existing facilities, here is my tried-and-true, fully verified method for creating maximum leverage opportunities in self storage.

- Buy in a growing market with similar sized competition—avoiding markets with REIT or institutional ownership is ideal but may not always be possible. This could be third tier or second tier, possibly fourth tier if you are confident it's growing. Basically, what defines a good opportunity is an area with years of steady growth and a diverse employer base that's also growing. You want a place people want to move to.

- Buy from an individual owner, preferably one who is out of state and hasn't visited the site in a long time (years). However, there are also opportunities if they live locally or even if they are the on-site manager. What you're looking for is a hands-off owner, one that is not actively engaged in running the facility—and you can almost always tell if this is the case.

- Look for these characteristics in your first facility purchase:
  - Good location (this can't be fixed).
  - Not good curb appeal (this *can* be fixed).
  - Not utilizing technology like the competition (online presence, marketing, and other things to streamline operations).
  - 100% occupancy, especially if they are charging below-market rates.
  - Lax management that cares more about being full than rocking the boat.
  - Low rental rates in comparison to the market.

- Manage it yourself (this does not mean you are there every day; this means you put all systems in place and don't hire a third-party management company to do it).

- As an alternative, hands-off management strategy, hire a top third-party management company. You should have run your numbers before making the purchase with this plan in mind so you know your margins will still be good.

- Hire all the personnel yourself and train them (most of the time you're not able to keep existing personnel because they have bad habits and often are the very reason the storage facility is performing poorly).
- Audit all the vendors. Make sure you don't have any long-term contracts and get the best vendors in place. Sometimes the existing vendors are friends of the owner or the owner didn't know any better when they hired them.
- Make changes immediately:
  - Raise rates to current to get rid of price-conscious tenants.
  - Collect on any unpaid rents.
  - Improve offerings, appearance, and showroom.
  - Put marketing strategy in place.

Other important aspects to know as you consider this approach:

1. Explore seller financing for the purchase; this can be a win-win for both sides and one more way to leverage your capital.
2. Most people don't evaluate self storage as a business, but as a real estate asset—they are not evaluating the potential revenue.
3. Don't buy on pro forma data (an analysis based on certain assumptions and projections)—such as the cap rate. Any cap rate calculation makes assumptions about revenue and expense ratios that will change when you take over the facility.
4. Banks and brokers can be good resources for finding deals, and especially for finding distressed properties.

> ## I don't let real estate agents tell me what something's worth and I don't let banks tell me what I can afford.

At the end of the day, this is about doing your own research and analysis.

I've already explained many of the reasons why this model works, but here is a summary:

- Takes advantage of the fragmented nature of the self storage industry (you can buy from an individual).
- Maximizes leveraging opportunities in these areas:
  - Technology (purchase a facility that is not using technology to their advantage and upgrade with website, PMS, security).
  - Curb appeal, offerings, and add-on services improvements will all increase revenue.
  - Type of tenants (purchase a facility that caters to price-conscious customers, upgrade it, raise rates to get rid of those tenants and attract quality-conscious customers who will pay more).
  - Your down payment investment (once you have maximized the valuation and revenue of your first property, you can use revenue collected, a line of credit, or refinance to get your down payment back to buy another).

BUYING VERSUS BUILDING VERSUS CONVERTING

Which approach is best for you depends on your goals, resources, and how you intend to operate the facility. Buying requires the smallest amount of capital and is a great way to enter the industry with the least amount of risk, and it can offer the greatest opportunity for leverage as a wealth vehicle. It's also the best way to learn the industry.

If you want to be completely hands-off and hire a third-party management company, you have to go big—these services generally do not operate in small markets and small facilities. If you don't want to have a manager, you should go small.

Building and converting do not have a built-in tenant base nor existing cash flow. So there's more risk that you don't fill up or that there's not enough demand in the market to make it work. It's more speculative in nature because you are assuming there will be more demand. Converting is top of mind for many because of all the big box commercial real estate that's sitting empty. If you can get them for under market value, that could be an opportunity. I'll cover some important considerations for these other approaches to give you a starting point.

Building and converting also require careful market research and competitor tracking to make the right decisions—just like buying an existing one.

IDENTIFY YOUR GOALS AND RESOURCES

People invest for different reasons and everyone has their own level of comfort with risk.

Are you trying to build a real estate empire or are you trying to get a small amount of cash flow to cover a house payment? Are you looking for a way to diversify and do just one deal? How much risk are you willing to take on? Do you want to be involved in the business, or be completely hands-off? The answers to these questions will help you decide whether you should buy or develop, self-manage or hire outside managers, and what markets you should go into.

Remember, you're creating a wealth vehicle to take you to financial freedom. But the road to financial freedom is different for all of us. So you need to make sure your wealth vehicle is the appropriate one to travel on your path.

I came up with a personal wealth calculator when I was in my twenties because I was trying to define where I wanted to go. I researched this and everybody talked about "financial freedom" but they didn't really define it—they just talked about numbers.

They would ask, "What's your freedom number?" It sounded just like the amount of money you need to retire. There are many blog posts on this. I came up with my own standard using three different levels:

1. Financial security
2. Financial independence
3. Financial freedom

These three levels are distinct. Financial security means you don't go bankrupt. You can pay your bills and put some food in your mouth. Right? But other than that, you can't even watch Netflix. You're just surviving.

Financial independence means you replace your income. But that may not mean you're traveling to Hawaii or something.

You may say to yourself, "Okay. I've got $3,000 a month. I can cover my bills. I can go to the park with my dog and go to the movies. I can do basic stuff. But it's not at all where I imagine being in life." You're above surviving, but you're really not thriving.

Financial freedom is a number that means you are free to do whatever you like. That concept and amount of money is different for everyone.

You may know a person who says, "Listen. I want to live in a cabin in the mountains and I'm happy to stay there." But the financial freedom number is everything that is included within that. This is important for somebody to understand.

If someone says, "I'm trying to protect my downside and that's it." Okay, let's calculate that. Add up all your debts, add up the exact cost to pay for your house or whatever it may be and that's what you need to replace.

Someone else may want to replace their income so they can do other things. In order to continue to grow and progress to a higher level, not only do you need to be creating enough money so you can live, but you also need capital to reinvest.

You need to include the capital you need in the financial planning because you can't just keep draining. You need the passive income coming in consistently to pay bills, but if you want to grow your income, if you want to build wealth, you need a plan for how you will do that. Where's the capital for the next deal coming from?

Most end up getting another job! Or they realize they just bought themselves a job, and that's what I tell everybody to avoid. That's not getting off the treadmill.

Don't invest in a job. Lots of people do this with storage. "Here's my number," and then suddenly, every day they're running a storage facility. At that point they realize they are not actually financially free at all. If they stop, they don't make money.

So you have to understand your goals with self storage. If you just want to have some side income, you probably just want to invest with other people.

If you can, start in a midsize facility because it's easier to achieve the margins and provide the personalized service of an on-site manager and the technology than in a smaller facility where margins are tighter. Small facilities are more accessible in terms of capital but be careful that it's not a shrinking market and that there's room for an on-site manager in the margin, if you don't want to be that person yourself.

If you have some capital, experience, and ambition, start bigger. Start with midsize facilities in maybe a little bigger market, with healthy demand and high revenue per SF. The key to this is to start in the best, most favorable situation that you can.

If you're trying to build a real estate empire, you probably don't want to stay in third-tier markets, even if that's where you start. You need to move up. Why? Because you need velocity of money—you need acceleration. But you still start there and then move up to bigger markets. But you need to get out of there quickly and then that gets you accelerating your money.

> ## In order to start the right way and choose the right facility, you need to know what you want from your first self storage business— which means knowing what's next.

This is true whether you buy, build, or convert. The playbook for these approaches to getting started in the industry varies only a little, however, and doing your due diligence is the same: you need to understand your markets and competition. I have seen more than one facility built from the ground up that couldn't pay the bills because they didn't analyze the market before choosing to build, and they chose an overbuilt market.

Building from the ground up will not usually make sense in an overbuilt market. Being in that market might work, depending on the competition and if you buy an existing one in foreclosure from the bank—but not if you are footing the construction costs. I caution you to always evaluate the local market before investing through any route. Buying in a bad market is the quickest way to lose money. If you aren't certain it's a good market, don't risk it and keep looking. You want to see clear signs that the area has the growth and demand you are looking for.

Finding the right market is step one for any approach.

Your resources include the capital you have available to invest, the financing capability you have or are willing to create, and other resources—including your business network and connections. You may see a way to purchase an empty big-box store location that could be a great location for a fully automated, climate-controlled self storage facility. If you have the amount of capital needed to do it, conversion could be the best way for you to go, once you understand your markets and rates.

If you own a contracting business and want to diversify, developing could be a cost-effective route for you.

What Is OPM?
OPM is other people's money. This could be any lender including a bank, a family member, or a friend. Any money that's not your own. The bigger the purchase is, the more likely you are to need OPM from someone to swing it.

The information I provide in this book and through the resources at SelfStorageIncome.com can help you reduce your risk in investing in the self storage industry. You will understand how the industry works and can avoid many mistakes. My Self Storage Facebook and Instagram groups are another resource. I encourage you to join those groups to start educating yourself.

But you still need to know what you want from the investment (extra income, a wealth vehicle), how hands-on you want to be in managing it (on-site manager, hands-on management setup, or completely hands-off), and how much of your own capital and how much OPM (other people's money) you are comfortable working with. These things will help you to define what kind of facility you want to own and how you want to acquire it—buy existing, build, or convert.

IDENTIFY A MARKET AND RESEARCH IT

Understanding the markets and how to evaluate a region and then a local market is the first step, regardless of how you plan to enter the business. One of the real opportunities in the self storage industry is that the market for each location is very localized; the customers for any location are within a five-mile radius of the facility. So if you drive around and see too many self storage locations in one area, move on to another area. It may be completely underserved and a great opportunity.

But it's more than simply the number of facilities; you need to know what kind of storage products they offer, how they are operating the business, what level of technology they are using, what they charge, and what their occupancy rate is. If all of the competition is older facilities with no online presence, that's an opportunity.

If you don't understand demand and market rates in your area, you may never recover your investment. You have to know if other self storage units are being built at the same time or are in the planning stages.

Starting in too small a market can be just as risky as starting in a market dominated by REITs. Too small and you have no options—especially if the local economy centers around only one or two major employers. A market with only a few thousand people is extremely risky. If that population is stagnant or even shrinking, your risk of losing money is high, no matter how you set it up.

What you need, regardless of the local population, is a growing, expanding population and stabilized with a diverse employer base that has also been growing for a while. And it needs to have been growing consistently for a while.

The details of how to do market research are in the valuation chapter.

BUYING

The playbook that's included in the Introduction (also see my podcast on this at https://www.podbean.com/media/share/pb-xhaye-cbf04a) is based on buying existing facilities. That's because lowest risk is in purchasing something with a known revenue. It is also the method requiring the smallest amount of capital.

There are many advantages to buying as your entry into the self storage market, and it's where my value-add strategy provides the most leverage.

If you want to enter the market by buying an existing facility, you need to know two things:

- How much money you have to invest
- How you plan to manage it—yourself, or hire a third-party management company

The answers define what kind of facility you should look for and will narrow your search considerably. If you don't know these two things, you may end up with the wrong thing and it may not produce what you want.

Once you know what kind of facility you want to buy, find one that's focused on price conscious tenants and upgrade it to appeal to quality-conscious tenants. You can increase the revenue by up to 100% in this manner, depending on the market.

WHO IS BUYING SELF STORAGE?

As I mentioned earlier, the self storage market is consolidating but that is still in the early stages. Because the big players are looking in first-tier markets and at bigger facilities to buy, there are many opportunities left to find. So who is buying self storage? Here's how the buyer profiles (segments) are, as I write this book:

1. **REITs:** These are $40B storage companies with big assets. There are about five of them and they are fighting to compete with others and gain market share. It's important to know if they are in your area because they are using sophisticated marketing practices to gain market share.

2. **Midsize:** Companies that own two to ten or more facilities. These are regional and even national, up to 200 facilities. They are intermediate players.

3. **Single ownership:** This market is massive—it's a huge percentage of the market, around 70%. This is where the opportunity lies. There are lots of markets where you can start out and be competitive. You can do competitor tracking and studies to find your competitors. Most of the one-offs are either high net worth individuals or individuals running a single establishment.

Find out where you fit into this mix. Are you looking for one or maybe two facilities as an income or retirement strategy, or are you looking to expand and acquire several and create a portfolio of facilities? This will affect how you buy and where you choose to purchase.

THE ROAD MAP FROM $200K TO $4M

One of the first self storage facilities my partners and I bought was a $200K investment on a $665K purchase out in the middle of nowhere near the Canadian border in Idaho. This was a fourth- or maybe a fifth-tier market, which in this case means there are more grizzly bears than people. It's a beautiful place.

The storage facility didn't have an office—it was more of an outpost. No gate, just five open buildings. We bought it and ran it for a few years and sold it later for $625K—a loss of $40K. It did have some cash flow, and in running it we learned where the opportunities were.

That's the important lesson from our first purchase—we learned. There was no playbook. We learned what we needed and what to do to make money, and that location wasn't it. When we realized that, we sold it for a small loss and used a 1031 exchange to buy our next facility, a 40K SF location for which we paid $1.4M with $290K down.

We picked this facility because of everything we had learned. The value-add opportunity was there—it had the rate discrepancies, it needed improvement, it had bad management. But it was a small facility. We bought it and in just over a year, we increased rates, turned it around, did the management ourselves because it was a smaller facility—and we sold it for $2.2M. We netted $1M from that investment, and it wasn't the result of market appreciation. It was value added through our management.

Immediately, we used another 1031 exchange to put our $1M down on a 70K SF facility that we paid $3.6M for. Currently we are expanding that one and two years later, it is worth nearly $8M. Our $200K is now $4M (we increased the value of that facility by $4M).

That was four years ago. And the cash flow each year from the 70K SF facility is more than the original $200K we invested in northern Idaho. That's the power of the strategy.

HOW TO LOOK FOR YOUR FIRST PURCHASE

Value is based on price, convenience, and quality. You want to buy a facility that competes on price and upgrade it to compete on quality. Convenience is about location—always look at location because this is the one thing you can't change.

Look for a facility in a market you can compete in—ideally with no or few large self storage owners/operators or REITs. However beware of too small a market, as I have mentioned.

Search "storage" online in that market—if nothing shows up or the online presence is limited, and there are in fact storage facilities in that area . . . go to that market.

I'll cover how to research the market more in the valuation chapter, but here's an overview. You want to "secret shop" facilities in your chosen market:

- Gather rate information
- Confirm there is high occupancy to confirm demand
- Look for upside/value add

Identify the facility in your chosen market with the lowest
firm its occupancy—it should be high but if it's not, look deeper
can see why.

Then identify the facility in your chosen market with the highest rate
confirm that it also has high occupancy.

Determine the spread between the lowest-rate and highest-rate facility:

Why is there a spread? Answer that based on your observations.

How much would it take to create quality in the lowest-rate facility, in the same range as the highest-rate facility? Meaning, how much would it cost to get the lower rate/lower quality facility up to the higher rate/higher quality facility? Think new management software, paving, new employees, etc.

Beware of Speculative Construction in Self Storage

Just as contractors will build "spec" homes in a hot housing market, construction contractors will build a self storage facility without any intention of operating it—their sole intention is to sell it. They will build it and when it's completed, they will sell it with the certificate of occupancy (CO), meaning it's ready to open for business *but* it's never actually been open. This is real estate hot potato—because they haven't done their due diligence to be sure the demand for what they are building is there. As a general rule, I recommend you do not buy these. Not only have they not analyzed supply and demand, they haven't analyzed what types of storage the market *wants* in terms of types and sizes of units. It is pure, 100% speculation and can devastate markets. The same market we built our facility in, five years later had almost 1M SF being built this way.

You may also find facilities with only partial occupancy. Make sure you ask plenty of questions to find out how long they've been there.

Reach Out to the Seller

Contact the owner of your chosen facility and ask to meet:

- Ask why they got into storage.

been operating it and what its occupancy is

contractors who want to sell without ever

e owner.

lans to invest in storage.

y their facility. This is a great opportunity

nancing.

them to, purchase your facility. There are

on this approach, but this is the main idea and the core of the value-add strategy. The concept of an acquisition funnel, starting with finding the market and narrowing to the opportunity and the seller who wants to negotiate with you, will be covered in the next chapter.

CASE STUDY: EXISTING FACILITY VALUE-ADD PURCHASE

This is a classic value-add story. We found this deal through a combination of a broker relationship and going out on our own. The broker told us about the asset but didn't go talk to the owner. The seller, who built the facility, was never going to work with a broker. We went and knocked on the owner's door. We worked with him and got him to sell to us. It came with extra space in the center and some frontage land.

Even though the broker didn't negotiate the deal, we paid him a commission anyway—this was about maintaining a relationship with this person because he did enable the deal. We didn't have to pay him, but we did. He deserved it.

The owner/builder didn't know what he was doing when he built the facility. It was 100K SF facility. The manager was working part time and they weren't able to pay the bills. They had 300 5 x 5 units, and they were never going to be able to fill those. That's one of the mistakes the builder made—he didn't research supply and demand.

We bought it for $2.3M and put $800K into it. We reconfigured all the units—put in 10 x 10 and 10 x 20 units, cleaned it up, ripped out the front and put $100K into that alone, including security cameras. (The cameras that were there were actually fake.) We repaved it and filled it up quickly with quality-conscious tenants. We expanded it to 150K SF.

Originally it was at $0.26 per SF and we managed it up to $0.60 per SF per month. We put in good managers, policies, and procedures. We could expand the facility more, if we wanted to. That facility was worth over $10M, a few years later. Not only has it paid us back, we could probably go out and buy five or six more with the proceeds.

BUILDING

Building is one way to enter a self storage market, but you've got to know your market. I know, I keep saying this but I've seen too many builders make this mistake because there is an aspect to building that is speculative. It seems many of the decisions to build are made on hype. It's like chasing after a dream, and the more hype a city has about their economy and growth, the more self storage builders are the cause of their own demise. To avoid the hype, look at the numbers of existing demand first—not future demand—and know your costs.

Development always comes with greater risk, but we have used this approach in the past with success. We still use it today and always want to have development projects going on at any given time. Although we also acquire facilities, we want development in the mix because the lower risk associated with acquired facilities helps us offset the risk for development. That way we still get large increases in equity once that development is stabilized, and it can then be refinanced to give us a boost in capital to reinvest into our self storage business.

When deciding to build, first look at the consumers' needs and the operational needs of the business, not your own. Understanding your market with a service-oriented mindset is the first step to long-term success.

CASE STUDY: BUILDING WITHOUT DUE DILIGENCE

Here's an example: Someone built a half a mile away from us. It cost him $12M to build. We had the top rates in the entire city, were in a very similar kind of facility to his, and had a better product. Ours included a big showroom and cost us $3M. I don't know how he's going to pay the bills. We came in at fractions of the cost that people are coming in at today. We've already had people call us and ask us to buy them and we had to tell them we wouldn't buy them for that price. We bought from banks and brokers for less then what they had into it and we'll do it again. It's a hard situation, but they did it to themselves. And that's why, now, in an overbuilt market, the biggest threat in self storage is itself: the self storage industry.

WHY WOULD YOU BUILD A STORAGE FACILITY?

Building a storage facility can offer enormous upside in expensive, tight markets. In markets that have extreme high demand but no one wants to sell, building is often the only option for entering that market. For those with experience and understanding of the costs, how to evaluate markets, and how to underwrite the storage facility's financial performance, they can capitalize on these underserved markets.

As an example for one of our building projects, about five years ago we built in a market that was extremely underserved at the time. We bought the land and built for $3.5M and when we opened it up, we had lines of people out the door to rent our units. We were full within months and have been raising rates ever since. That facility today, even conservatively, would sell for more than $8M.

While those numbers seem extremely enticing, remember we built that facility five years ago. Today, that same market is completely overbuilt, and we would not build in that market at all. We've moved to other cities that have extremely tight markets and are difficult to enter for our recent building projects. The supply in those markets has remained low and is below 8 SF per capita.

The market from our development four years ago is now over 26 SF per capita.

How can you be successful in developing a storage facility? Develop where there's high demand *right now*. And develop where there's high demand on a good location and provide superior products and customer service. Obviously analyzing demand is part of your research, no matter how you decide to enter the market or where. See the details about demand in chapter 4 (The Art of Valuation and Finding Deals) under the heading Understanding Value Creators and Destroyers.

Another important piece of that puzzle is understanding what a customer is worth to you—are they worth $900 or $2,000? And how much does it take for you to acquire and keep that customer? You need to understand the *lifetime value* of your customers, which is part of managing your revenue and is covered in detail in the operations chapter. This also ties into your marketing budget, your upselling strategies, and your product offerings.

As the self storage real estate market tightens and acquisitions become harder to find at the right price, many owners and investors are looking at new development. This can be overwhelming for someone new to the industry.

Building comes with many challenges, but the first is to understand market demand and the right product to fill it. How to do this is covered in the chapter on valuation. You will understand more about supply and demand, and what kind of risks you are taking on, after you have done your due diligence research.

My partners and I have built from scratch and been successful—but it wasn't our first or our second facility. We didn't have a playbook back then. You need to know what you're doing before you build and you need to realize the time and capital it will take. From buying the land to stabilization of that asset will most likely be years.

One of the biggest advantages of my playbook for entering the market by buying an existing facility first is that you can learn how to play with less risk. So if you want to start by developing your own facility, make sure your team includes third-party vendors who specialize in self storage to give you a leg up on the competition and some of the knowledge you don't have.

The self storage industry is becoming more competitive and larger operators have scaling advantages. The business is also progressing to accommodate changing consumer needs, views, and expectations.

If your research shows an underserved market, that may be the opportunity you need. It's important to understand the existing demand as well as the future demand by knowing if any new storage projects are in the pipeline to be developed, and where. Work with the city and utilize data aggregation tools so you know where land around you can be changed to the right zoning in the future, if it doesn't have the correct zoning now. You want to know what else is coming on the market by the time you open. You also don't want to learn, a year after you open, that a massive storage facility is being built in a nearby cornfield that will completely alter demand in your market.

You need to have a specific plan for finding and serving your customers, and you need to focus on understanding the market's demand and pricing. All of this needs to be part of your ROI and revenue projection analysis.

QUESTIONS TO ASK BEFORE COMMITTING TO BUILDING

Before jumping in, ask yourself these questions:

1. How Will You Attract New Customers?

Location is the number one thing that has to be right. In the twenty-first century, you actually have two locations to manage: your physical property and your online presence. Both need to be set up to effectively attract new tenants.

For the physical property, population density and traffic count are large indicators of whether your new venture will be successful. Focus on a three-mile radius around your facility, as this is where you'll attract a majority of your customers.

The internet has surpassed other methods for attracting new tenants. Your website must be mobile-friendly, easy to navigate, and answer the questions your ideal tenant is asking. Attracting new customers is more than having a great website, however. Your marketing strategy (SEO and pay-per-click strategies) must be geared toward that ideal tenant.

2. How Will You Serve New Customers?

The operation you put in place and the manager in charge of your facility will create your customer experience. Your facility must be easy to access and provide services your target market requires. Online payments, 24-hour access, security, conference rooms, Wi-Fi, RV dumps, climate control, unit lighting, and an easy-to-navigate entrance and exit are just a few of the many services that need to be addressed when designing a competitive product.

3. What Are Your Options for Ingress and Egress?

High traffic is a main goal, but ease of entrance and exit can be a major issue for you and your customers. Make sure your driveways and parking accommodate incoming and outgoing traffic. You'll need more parking during your fill-up phase than when your facility becomes stabilized.

4. What's Your Value Proposition?

Your services, location—online and offline—staffing, quality, and unique unit sizes will all go into your value proposition. Look at how your development will differentiate itself in the market. The self storage industry must be approached as an active business, not a passive real estate investment. It needs to have many of the qualities that retail companies strive to achieve.

Your facility must be enticing to new customers, and it needs to look and feel welcoming, safe, and efficient, both physically and operationally. The build of your store must coincide and reflect the operation of your business. Think about the customers' needs and how they'll use your product. This will dictate how you build your property.

As the industry grows and customers are more familiar with self storage services, their needs and wants are becoming more diverse. They expect more product options as well as more services to come with those options.

If you're trying to capture the demand for RV units, for example, you need to build with that in mind. If you want your facility to have plentiful outdoor and indoor parking for RVs, the size of the lanes is critical. If they aren't wide enough, it can be too difficult to get in and out of the property. This can also lead to damage to your buildings. It's vital you think about these details as you design your facility.

5. Will You Offer Climate Control?

If you're focusing on climate-controlled units, look hard at what tenants are storing and consider any other accommodations that should be made. Many tenants are using climate-controlled units for specific reasons, such as collectibles and medical inventory. Available power, lighting, and increased security may be the differentiation you need.

6. Who Is Your Target Tenant and Why Do They Need Your Product?

Climate control, outdoor parking, and unit size can vary greatly, depending on your market and population density. Make sure you build a product that's not only right for your market but won't contribute to oversaturation.

7. Do You Want to Attract Businesses?

Catering to specific tenants can be a profitable strategy if the demand is there. Look at the industries in your area and their storage needs. Many contract workers need a place to store their inventory and supplies. Others may need a place to conduct business.

We had one facility that was specifically designed to attract businesses, so we made larger aisleways to allow businesses in and out with semitrucks. We sacrificed some square footage, but we were able to make up for that with higher prices and steady, long-term customers.

8. What Ancillary Services Could Make Your Facility More Valuable?

Try to offer your tenants something your competitors aren't. Before you build, go to the market and test it. The best way to analyze your market and the competitors is to obtain a feasibility study. It's important it's done by someone who's familiar with the storage industry and the unique challenges that come with it. Also, get out and visit the facilities around your proposed site to see what's already being offered. How will your facility and services fit in the market?

9. Will You Manage It Yourself or Hire a Third-Party Management Company?

The greatest leveraging opportunity, not to mention learning opportunities, come from managing it yourself. And this means setting up the systems and hiring and training the manager yourself, not putting on the uniform and being there every day. However, one of the beautiful things about self storage as an investment is you can choose to be completely hands off and hire a third-party company to do it for you. You'll find critical information to help you, either way you want to go, in the operations chapter later in the book.

YOU NEED A DREAM TEAM

You need an awesome team around you to help you succeed in self storage—a team that's experienced in self storage so they can make sure everything's done right. Also have a feasibility study done by a third party to confirm or contradict your assumptions about the location where you intend to build. Then you need a builder who's experienced in the self storage space to help you through the process. And if you're not experienced, you need an experienced operator who can look at things and say, "This doesn't make sense."

One of the main things I see when people build self storage that doesn't make sense is the showroom or office space is either too small or it's inside the facility. Why would you put the office inside the gate? In order to have potential customers walk in to see you, the gates have to be open and now you're no longer secure. Your secure facility can't be secure and open at the same time with the office inside the facility. So the office needs to be outside the gate and available to the public to walk in. And the office should have an entrance into the secure facility so existing customers can access it either through the office or through the gate with their code.

FOCUS ON THE CONSUMER'S NEEDS

Remember you are building a business, not a real estate asset. When you develop self storage, you need to focus on the consumer's needs and think about how they will utilize your facility. How will they access the unit? Do they need to drive a truck up to their unit? Who are they—businesses, individuals? What unit types will you offer that they want and that will make them choose your facility over the competition? Wine storage, collectible vehicles storage? Do this before you start the project.

CASE STUDY: BUILDING A NEW FACILITY NEEDS TO BE A HOME RUN

For one of our first building projects, we identified a market that had almost no new inventory even though everything at the time was completely full and raising rates. Demand was sky-high in this market. We purchased a prime spot on a major five-lane road for an amazing price—under $3 per SF of land. When we analyzed the market in the three-mile radius, we found no one was offering climate-controlled, drive-up, or enclosed RV parking storage. At the time (approximately five years ago), prices were substantially less.

We knew we could build for under $50/SF. We built an 85K SF facility and the office was a large showroom—big enough to hold a small crowd—with vaulted ceilings and granite countertops.

When we opened it, we were told it was the JW Marriot of self storage. This was important because we stood out from our competition both in looks *and* offerings. As I described above, we had lines going out the door when we opened. The revenue stabilized in three months at over 80% occupancy. It was a complete home run.

The reason this project was so successful was a combination of high demand, reasonable cost, and product offerings that were not readily available in that area—and it was in a great location—not only was it on a major road with lots of traffic, it was close to two of the busiest intersections in the state and within a mile of an interstate interchange.

At first, we were nervous to build because of the additional risk that building has—we had constant questions about are we going to fill up and is this the right time, but we got comfortable and executed through thorough research and understanding of the economics and supply and demand in that area.

It was important for us to make sure we weren't being blinded by our own biases. Everyone has biases that make them think the location they choose will be great and people will love their product, but sometimes the market doesn't agree.

To make sure that didn't happen, we hired a third party to do a feasibility study to confirm or deny our results. When looking for the third party to do the study, it was important for us that they had expansive knowledge in the self storage industry, as well as were owners and operators of storage facilities. Once the results were confirmed, we felt confident to move forward.

If you are looking for a third party to do a feasibility study, find someone who specializes in self storage. No one else will have the right context or understanding of the industry and the markets. Real estate brokerage firms offer this type of service too but they are usually generalists and that will not do—you need someone who specializes in self storage.

For us, building a new self storage facility has to be a complete home run—not just good—or we won't touch it. New construction always has added risk because you are changing the supply/demand in the area *plus* you are guessing that there is actually demand there. Only if it's a home run will you have the margin of safety you need.

CONVERTING

You can enter the self storage market by converting an existing building. You have to have a lot of capital and knowledge to do this—so for the large majority of investors, this is not the way to start. Permitting and working with the city to accomplish this is a big task and for the first conversion we did, we had a partner who knew how to do this.

The retail evolution (apocalypse) that is happening right now is leaving a trail of empty big-box commercial real estate buildings that can be perfect for this—in the right location and market. The research for this kind of deal is the same as if you were buying, with a little bit different input for your value proposition and deal analysis.

Something we look at when evaluating these locations is whether it's a stand-alone building or connected to other businesses. If it's connected to other businesses, you have to deal with leases from other people and guidelines that apply to all of them. It can be done but it adds a layer of complexity—and if the leases from the other people don't allow a storage business usage for the site, then you can't convert it.

Conversions can sometimes take longer than normal development due to working with the city and the seller. During the writing of this book, we were in the middle of a conversion in a market that had less than 6 SF per capita of self storage, in a bankrupt Sears on the main road. The building had been sitting empty for a few years. At this point, the seller was willing to come down on price and the city, who had an anti-storage attitude up to that point, was coming around and was willing to entertain the idea because they didn't want an empty building.

This offered advantages to us. First, we could get into a building and make it climate controlled. We had enough square footage on a main road with signage that we probably couldn't have gotten otherwise. If the building hadn't been vacant and the city hadn't hated it so much, they wouldn't have let us build a storage facility there. So it offered a unique opportunity to get into a high-demand market.

DON'T OVERLOOK BIG EXPENSES

You need to be careful with conversions. Just because you're converting something that's unoccupied doesn't necessarily mean it's a good deal. You need to look at the cost of building a similar facility from scratch. You need to understand, first of all, if it's cheaper to build a storage facility from the ground up than it is to buy an empty building and convert it, in the exact same area and market. Also, you need to understand if the opportunity to build in that area even exists (if there aren't any opportunities to build, then the conversion is an opportunity). *And* you need to know if there's enough demand for what you want to do.

The big things you need to look out for are capital expenditures, when evaluating a conversion. Roofs, HVAC, and cement. Sometimes these facilities need the roof or the HVAC system replaced, not just repaired. These are huge dollar items, in the hundreds of thousands, that are not associated with building from the ground up.

Our latest roof replacement on a conversion project cost us $800,000. You don't want to buy a problem (especially a surprise problem), so make sure the existing infrastructure is good and functional—or understand the cost and the time frame in which repairs can be completed and build that into your plan.

The facility will also need an office and building entrances and exits that work for the kind of storage you plan to provide, not to mention the storage units themselves. You need to truly understand the all-in cost of what you're buying. The price plus the cost to be operational—and that's just the existing structure without the conversion process to storage. Just the box itself.

Look carefully at how people will access the location, how they will get in and out, and the street frontage. How the vehicles will work for loading/unloading and parking. In our old Kmart conversion, we blew the side walls out and made a drive aisle. So people can drive through the facility and park inside the facility to access their units. This required special HVAC systems as well as doors to allow people in and out and to take care of the exhaust. These are all extra expenditures that need to be included in your analysis of whether to go for it or not—the specifics for what will be needed to make it work.

FOCUS ON DEMAND

Just like any other way to enter a self storage market, you've got to focus on demand and utilization.

QUESTIONS TO ASK BEFORE COMMITTING TO A CONVERSION

1. What would the cost be to buy the building and make it fully operational (just the shell)?
2. Can the competition build new storage facilities around you, and is it cheaper to build from the ground up than it is to convert?
3. What is the advantage of converting versus building? If the market has demand and no other available space to build nearby, that could be the opportunity. You need to clearly understand that.

4. What would it cost to convert to storage units, including access for loading/unloading, a nice office/showroom, and parking?
5. What is current demand and SF per capita of available storage in the area?
6. Is the city government open to allowing what you need to do?

CASE STUDY: FORMER SUPER KMART CONVERSION

Conversion can be a great option if you have the capital. We had bought numerous existing facilities and also developed self storage from the ground up before we did this deal. It was a networking deal, through connections we made from our self storage co-op organization called StoreLocal. StoreLocal is a group of independent self storage players who pool their resources to be able to access opportunities—such as great vendor contracts—that are otherwise only available to the big players.

Through StoreLocal, I've met several potential partners. One loved my philosophy for how we did things, and he offered me an opportunity to work on a deal with him concerning a bankrupt Super Kmart. He was local and worked with the city to get the right permitting to get it zoned for a storage facility. I was interested in the market and the location looked good. We purchased that empty Super Kmart building for $6M. We sold the parking lot to a multifamily developer. At that point we had $3M into it. We put in a $5M bid that included implementing all the automation technology—everything from remote access to wireless access from a mobile phone.

We were charging an average of over $1.00 per SF. We hadn't been operating it for a full year when someone approached us and asked if they could buy that facility for over $20M. We said no . . . but imagine what it will be in five years.

This is a huge indoor facility that is completely automated, although we do have staff because of its size. You never have to talk to somebody to use it. In all, it was an $8M build and it's now a $20M asset, not counting the annual revenue. That deal was the combination of everything we had learned and great partners.

KEY TAKEAWAYS

- ▶ There are multiple ways to enter the industry, and which one is right for you depends on your goals and resources.
- ▶ For many people, the best approach is to buy your first one and learn the ropes: evaluate your local market, find the underperforming ones for sale, purchase the right one, upgrade it with facilities and technology, and run it.
- ▶ After you're established and have learned the industry, other ways to enter a new market make more sense. Building and converting could be stepping-stones on your path to an empire.

CHAPTER 4

The Art of Valuation and Finding Deals

No matter how you intend to enter the self storage industry (buy, build, convert), you need to know how to value a facility. The value is based on a facility's *revenue potential* and on the risk involved—these are the keys. It's not about the asking price—value and price are not the same. Efficient market theory does not work here. You need to define the value based on what you are looking for. We are buying a real estate asset that has revenue and expenses.

Value and price are not the same!

The revenue potential is based on the local market and local competition and also on how the facility is being managed. The risk also relates to the market and competition, potential fluctuations in demand, and known performance of competitors. This is where your due diligence comes in. You have to do three things:

1. Evaluate the revenue potential of a facility you want to buy, based on the current competition and the state of the market—current rates and occupancies and whatever upside you see for your value-add strategy.

You have to know or estimate your expense ratio for operating the facility in order to do this.

2. Evaluate your ability to execute on your value-add strategy. This includes knowing how you intend to manage the facility (and the resulting expense ratio), how you will manage its revenue, and how you will market it to realize that potential.

3. Evaluate the risk involved. How stable are the cash flows (if you are buying an existing facility) and how predictable will they be in the future (demand)?

UNDERSTANDING VALUE CREATORS AND DESTROYERS

Evaluation of the potential and the risk in any self storage investment requires an understanding of the *value creators* and also the *value destroyers* that can drive and affect the revenue potential and risk. Every situation will have nuances and individual characteristics that you need to evaluate.

Once you have a good understanding of value creators and destroyers, you need to **look at them in terms of what you can control and what you can't**— so you choose projects with the right things from the start (those things you can't control). I've already mentioned location as an example of something you can't control—so it has to be good for any project you choose. Competitive advantage and opportunity may be in your control and may be leverage points.

> ## Understand clearly what you can fix (or choose to do correctly, for development or conversions) and what you can't.

Don't try to fight an upstream battle. Your valuation of any project should focus on what you can't control first and eliminate those projects with the wrong characteristics before you waste any more time on them.

Here are the value creators I look for when I'm evaluating any deal:

- Demand
- Opportunity
- Competitive advantage
- Demographics
- Markets and what's happening, i.e., debt markets, real estate business cycle

Value destroyers include a shrinking or stagnating economy (overall and local) and oversupplied storage in the market. So it's the flipside of the opportunity, when things are not favorable. For instance, the national economy could be booming but in a small area if a local employer closes down, that local economy will go into a slump because unemployment will rise and real estate values will drop.

SUPPLY AND DEMAND

Demand is, if not *the* most important thing to evaluate, it's *one* of the most important things. It will make you or break you, and at a certain point, no operator—no matter how good they are—can succeed in an oversupplied market. Don't try. Once you know that about a potential project, put away your pride if it's involved, and move on.

How do we analyze demand? There are tools that help you to do this (data aggregator software), but no tool is perfect. Understanding supply and demand can be both a science and an art. I hear lots of different benchmarks like this one: after 8 SF per capita, the market is starting to get overbuilt. I can tell you that's not a hard-and-fast rule.

That number only tells part of the story. I know markets that have 8 SF per capita and are overbuilt and then I know markets that have 14 SF per capita and still have tremendous demand. So you need to analyze and assess how many SF per capita a market can hold or sustain. But if there's no firm rule on SF per capita, how do you determine if 8 SF per capita is too much for a market and it's oversupplied? Or can that market sustain 15 SF per capita?

As a general rule, over 10 SF per capita should be a cause for concern in a particular market. With that said, understand that there are markets with higher square footage that still have a lot of demand. **So no matter what SF per capita number you find, don't take it at face value.**

What we generally see is a compression of prices trending with the more square footage there is in the market. And that makes sense.

But you need to confirm the SF per capita with occupancy rates in the storage facilities. You need to overlay what's happening with occupancy by different types of units in the storage facilities with the market demand. And to do that, you need to do some footwork. Phone calls first, but you need to walk into the showroom of every facility in the market and talk to the manager—as a customer. This is a critical part of your research and will also tell you who is a good operator and who's not. You need to know who's good to really get a true picture of the supply and demand. And identifying who's underperforming might indicate an opportunity for you to acquire.

I've been in markets with 8 SF per capita and when talking with the managers, found that they could get me into almost any unit. I've been in markets with 12 SF per capita where the manager told me they wouldn't even put me on a waiting list because so many people were already waiting that I'd never get in.

Understanding how the people in that three-mile or five-mile radius are consuming and which units they are consuming, is critical. Remember, those units are different products. In the West, people tend to go for bigger units. The 10 x 20s are a hit. In the Northeast, they like smaller units. You need to understand the demand for each type of storage and the sizes available within each category. I've already listed these—climate controlled, drive-up, parking, the size of each, etc.

We'll cover more on evaluating the competition in the next chapter.

What the competition is doing will tell you what kind of demand exists at that moment in the market. If they have vacancies and are dropping prices, that's a key sign that markets are oversupplied. But if they've had steady rate increases year-over-year and have little inventory, that indicates demand.

Find out the occupancy for each type of unit at each facility. Are they completely full? Only climate controlled are full, and everything else is at 50%? When even the bad operators are completely full and have long wait times, that's a good sign. I also look at price increases and especially if they've been increasing prices for a long time and they are still full.

> ## At the end of the day, you're trying to answer a simple question: How much SF per capita can this market handle?

The best way to understand that, once you have the existing SF per capita and have overlaid it with the competition's occupancy rate, is to evaluate the competition and the overall growth of the city, the demographics, and also new supply coming onto the market.

FUTURE SUPPLY

To understand new supply that could come onto the market, you need to focus on two things: the government and the competition.

The government can help you understand where storage facilities can be built, what storage facilities are currently being built, and what may soon be developed. Understanding the pipeline of future supply is critical to understanding how safe your projected future revenues are.

That's why you have to be careful in small markets and why I usually avoid them. Everyone could be completely full and you build a 35K SF facility, and there's no one to fill it up. You need to look at what's being consumed and where the SF per capita is, and then you need to look at whether the city is growing. Are new people moving in? Are they renters or homeowners? What's the average income? What's the growth forecast for the city? Is there movement within the city, from one area to another? Is the real estate market moving well or is it stagnant? Stagnation is bad for self storage. I'm not saying you have to have a hot market, but it should be moving. Movement creates demand. You need a steady, growing, solid market that has activity.

OPPORTUNITY

There's a few things we look for to evaluate the opportunity. First, we look for a difference between what better operators charge and what underperforming operators charge. This shows you that the market is willing to pay better operators a premium. Then, we look for poor operators we can purchase. In that scenario, the opportunity could be to change the physical look of the facility, or it could be all in operational changes. If it's a run-down facility, it may need sprucing up and a better showroom. Or it could be all operational—maybe they're not raising their rates at all, or maybe they are 100% full but haven't raised rates in forever and they have 10% delinquencies. Maybe they're not marketing, or the manager is terrible. Maybe they've got the wrong offering mix.

COMPETITIVE ADVANTAGE

Look at all the competitors in a three-mile radius and understand how they are running their facilities. A great opportunity would be if they are running it like a real estate asset and not a business. There's no outreach, no churn. It's stagnant, and the manager is like a placeholder just waiting for people to come in.

Or if they are all amazing operators with great marketing strategies, you need to ask yourself, how will you compete? If you're not as good as they are, will that affect your income?

DEMOGRAPHICS

This ties back into demand. We like to see diverse demographics with a healthy middle class. Look for real estate prices and incomes rising over a long period of time.

STATE OF THE ECONOMIC MARKETS

The state of the markets—and by this we mean the economic situation on a bigger scale, not the local market—can create opportunities or erase them, as we have seen with the COVID-19 pandemic. The pandemic caused many to harbor cash and also to look for ways to deploy it into safer assets that aren't retail or hotels and can last through social distancing. Anything that's not dependent on walk-in traffic. Many were looking to invest in storage.

The other side of this was we were in a downturn—a recession—but prices didn't drop much. You still had to pay high prices to get into storage, and because the markets were in turmoil, financing was a big question. Financing options weren't predictable. You might not be able to get financing and if you did, would you get good terms?

So understanding what point of the business cycle you're in is very important in evaluating the future of your facility and your opportunity. You also want to build in a safety margin in case things slide after you've committed to a deal—make sure you can handle a 20% drop in revenue, for instance, without defaulting.

UNDERSTANDING CAP RATES

You buy based on what you can make something into—the potential you see from your own pro forma projections—but you don't pay somebody for that.

> ## Buy based on pro forma information but don't pay for it.

Cap rates are a benchmarking tool for some kinds of real estate investments. However, they don't work well in self-storage unless you calculate them for yourself. Cap rates don't determine value because the current cap rate doesn't tell you if a facility is a good buy or a bad buy. Cap rates are the wrong measure to use, bottom line.

I have bought facilities that were extremely undervalued at 5 caps and at 9 caps. That's because my method of valuation uses more than cap rates. I look at the underlying expenses due to management processes that directly affect the revenue the facility will produce. So it's a way of looking at the potential revenue based on what I know about operations and also on what I know about local supply and demand and the current performance of the competition, based on my own research of the local market.

However, understanding what a cap rate is and how to use it is part of the investing language. "Cap rate" is short for capitalization rate and it's a calculation used to analyze the rate of return for an asset, expressed as a percentage.

Capitalization Rate = Net Operating Income/Purchase Price

Cap rate is the ratio of net income to the price you paid. If you have net income of $100,000 and you paid $1M, that's a 10% cap rate. Cap rates are a way to measure the return you will get on your money. Investors often will shorten "10% cap rate" to "10 cap."

Also, if the cap rate is 10%, that means it will take you 10 years to recover your initial investment. You need to understand that the cap rate is calculated using a set of assumptions to come up with that NOI (net operating income) value—including the expense ratio and the revenue per SF.

If you have a 5 cap versus a 10 cap, the 10 cap is theoretically a much better investment than the 5 cap. Although that's not really true and it's not really how cap rates work.

What I use is a mix of the two approaches, and I don't call it a cap rate. Also, I never accept a cap rate valuation at face value. If you change the way a facility is managed, marketed, and how much you charge, the cap rate will change. Calculate your own cap rate based on your knowledge of costs and operational efficiencies and the upside in revenue management. I will show you how to do that as part of your evaluation of the investment potential for a self storage business.

Let's use an example of a 60K SF facility in a third-tier market.

- Facility: 60K SF
- Price: $2.8M
- Revenue: $360,000

- Expenses: $136,800
- NOI: $223,200
- Price/SF: $46.67
- Cap rate (face value): 7

Look at the price/SF in terms of its replacement cost—that is, what it would cost to build it. So a price/SF of $46.67 is low and indicates a great deal, especially by first-tier market standards, because the cost to build that facility would be more like $80/SF. However, the cap rate of 7% in a third-tier market seems low and therefore unattractive for that market because of the risk involved—lots of things can happen to that supply and demand that may be out of your control. You would want more like an 8 cap in that market, looking at it in the usual way.

So those two factors say two different things—the price/SF says it's a good deal but the cap rate says it's not. Why the discrepancy?

You have to look deeper—look at how that facility is being managed, current market rates and occupancies, and how you could increase revenue and decrease expenses with your own management methods—to determine if that's what the revenue, expenses, and resulting NOI would be if you were running it.

All of those elements are leveraging opportunities in self storage. The expenses alone can make a huge difference. On average, expenses in self-storage are around 35%. They don't change that much—as a general rule, they range from 28 to 40%. For a 50K SF facility, they are closer to the high end at 40-42, generally, and closer to 30% for a 100K SF facility. These are good numbers to have in hand when you evaluate a facility.

Managing that revenue, and whether it could go up or down, affects that value to you because the revenue you get is what makes it valuable to you. It's how much that asset is returning to you—your capital returns.

People's underlying assumptions about what is a good deal change, depending on an individual's circumstances and expectations. To one person, an 8% return out of a self storage facility may be a good deal. I wouldn't accept anything under 20% on a cash flow basis. I look at it on a cash flow basis, year to year. How much money am I going to make, how much will I have to put into it, and what's the risk associated with that? How fast can I get my money out?

In a third-tier market, the revenue isn't that secure (as a general rule) and the cap rate needs to be higher to balance that risk. That's the face value approach to looking at the cap rate. If you listen to my podcast or have seen some of my YouTube videos, you know how I feel about cap rates. Let me explain why that is.

The reason cap rates exist is because we value self storage based upon the revenue they bring in. What you need to understand is a cap rate encompasses a few variables, including revenue, expenses, and risk. So it sounds just like what you are looking for.

In theory, a lower cap rate means there's lower risk and the future revenues are more guaranteed. A larger cap rate means there's more risk, and so you get a higher return because the cash flows may not be as predictable in the future. But cap rates can vary wildly and most importantly, most of the cap rates I've ever seen are wrong.

They are wrong from the stance that the expenses are left out, revenue is overstated, or risk has not been properly evaluated on both ends. So for one property, you can have multiple people argue on the cap rate and what it equals.

That's why I don't look at any of those things. I look at the revenue and how it's being managed. If it's being mismanaged, that's an opportunity.

I would be happy to go into a 5 cap that has mismanaged revenue, where I can do a value-add process. I can change some of the revenue drivers, increase the revenue, and be more efficient with my expenses—and really drive the net income. That will increase my year-to-year cash flow.

That's how I find value. I look at the business operations and make sure they're effective. If the seller was doing a great job of maximizing revenue and you can't do as good a job or at least not any better, you're going to get hurt—because the value of self storage is based on the revenue.

> ## The value of a self storage facility is based on the revenue.

You need to know you can do a better job than the current operator and also not be outcompeted by someone with a bigger advertising budget.

However, it's not uncommon to find mismanagement, so you need to know what good management looks like. Revenue management will be covered in greater detail in the operations chapter, but a few things you can do to increase revenue include selling products besides the units themselves: insurance, boxes, and pallets. Also, how you manage the pricing of the different-sized units can have a huge impact on revenue. The supply and demand on the different sized units and the price per SF are different. That's where dynamic pricing can come into play with revenue management. You can manage it to achieve a peak capacity in terms of both occupancy and revenue per SF.

So how you should value self-storage is not so much on the cap rate as it is evaluating the existing expenses and revenue. Can you drive that revenue up? Is the revenue for that market known? Are the current expenses super high in a way that you won't have when you manage it?

	Year Ending 12/31/2019	Year Ending 12/31/2018	Year Ending 12/31/2017	Year Ending 12/31/2016
Gross Income				
Rental Income	671,800.00	635,400.00	563,500.00	437,800.00
Rental Income	9,600.00	10,200.00	9,100.00	5,300.00
Other Fees	14,700.00	15,400.00	14,800.00	800.00
Insurance Income	7,500.00	5,400.00	4,300.00	0.00
Moving Trucks	2,200.00	3,600.00	500.00	13,900.00
Merchandise Income	1,800.00	2,200.00	2,600.00	5,000.00
Merchandise COGS	(1,000.00)	(1,200.00)	(1,000.00)	(3,700.00)
Credits Issued	(21,100.00)	(23,600.00)	(9,900.00)	(1,500.00)
Total Gross Income	685,500.00	647,400.00	583,900.00	457,600.00
Operating Expenses				
Advertising and Promotion	27,000.00	18,800.00	22,400.00	4,400.00
Bank and Merchant Fees	12,900.00	13,300.00	10,700.00	9,600.00
Licenses, Permits, and Fees	100.00	100.00	100.00	100.00
Call Center	3,700.00	3,900.00	4,900.00	0.00
Computer, Support, and Software	5,800.00	6,100.00	4,600.00	900.00
Insurance Expense	4,700.00	5,300.00	5,500.00	6,000.00
Payroll	44,700.00	45,500.00	41,900.00	36,000.00
Postage, Freight, and Delivery	300.00	700.00	300.00	500.00
Professional Fees	2,200.00	3,000.00	2,300.00	1,500.00
Repairs and Maintenance	14,900.00	20,100.00	19,200.00	17,900.00
Security	500.00	2,200.00	5,400.00	2,400.00
Small Tools and Equipment	200.00	3,500.00	4,900.00	4,800.00
Supplies	2,100.00	1,800.00	6,600.00	4,900.00
Taxes	54,000.00	63,700.00	39,000.00	38,400.00
Telephone and Internet	1,800.00	3,100.00	1,900.00	5,300.00
Utilities	8,100.00	8,600.00	9,400.00	9,300.00
Bad Debt Expense	7,600.00	16,100.00	10,300.00	3,100.00
Total Operating Expenses	190,600.00	215,800.00	189,400.00	145,100.00
Net Operating Income	**494,900.00**	**431,600.00**	**394,500.00**	**312,500.00**

We purchased this location at the end of 2016 for a 7.8% cap. Through operational management changes only and zero capital expenditures, we increased this to a 12.3% cap and added $2.3M to our equity in three years.

UNDERSTANDING EXPENSE RATIOS: EVERY OPERATOR'S WILL BE DIFFERENT

The expense ratio is a critical part of any cap rate calculation. That ratio determines the expenses that will be subtracted from the revenue. Expenses are driven by the way you manage a business. Many decisions you make will affect your expenses and therefore your expense ratio.

One of the reasons you will learn so much about the industry through operating your first self storage facility, no matter what kind you choose, is that you will learn what your expense ratio is. Every operator's ratio will be different. Of course it's a ballpark with small changes based on site specifics, but you'll have a very good idea of where you stand after you've worked through it the first time.

You'll also learn about some of the expenses that are so often overlooked. Here's a list of expenses that get overlooked:

- Bad debt
- Cost of management (especially for owner/operators)
- Landscaping and snowplowing
- Capital expenses
- Taxes adjusted for the purchase price
- Advertising

For example, if you are looking at a facility that has very little online presence, whatever expenses they tell you they have for operating expenses will be lower than yours because they're not doing it effectively. So you need to know what each of these pieces will cost. I'll go into these in more detail because you need to understand what's involved to recognize how big an impact these could have on your revenue potential.

BAD DEBT

Many times in mom and pop facilities, owners are bad at collecting the rent. So you have a lot of units that may be occupied but the tenants aren't paying. That can be 10-15% of the facility. Simply cleaning that up can be a big boost to your revenue.

MANAGEMENT FEE

Often mom and pops don't include the cost of management because it's just them, their time—they're not counting that time and expense into the sheet. So whatever profit they calculate is not a true profit. Without knowing the cost of management, you could really overpay for a facility. Normal management fees can be anywhere from 4.5 to 6% of revenue but often third-party management companies will take the revenue from add-on products and insurance as another form of payment. They will say they charge 4.5% *but* they take the revenue from add-on products such as renters insurance so really their fee is 6%. That's a more standard estimate—6%.

LANDSCAPING AND SNOWPLOWING

This is an expense that many owners will leave out because they have a relative or one of their kids doing it. But these costs add up and are important to maintain the look of the facility, so it needs to be built in—and this can vary a lot, depending on the location and climate.

CAPITAL EXPENDITURES

This is the big daddy of where valuations go wrong. You may need to replace roofing, gates, or other things. Sometimes they are selling the facility because they don't want to address those issues. But it's part of acquisition and you need to understand what that project needs. This can be a make-it or break-it thing.

You can expect to have some capital expenditures with every purchase, but it's the big ones you need to watch out for. Because self storage facilities have so much paving, sealing of the pavement, just like roads, has to be done every three years on average. On most facilities we buy, resealing is a standard thing that has to be done when we buy.

PROPERTY TAXES

This is another really big one. How this is handled depends on local tax regulations and rates but normally, real estate taxes are tied to the valuation of the asset. If you are buying a facility that the owner built for $2M 25 years ago and you spend $5M for it, your taxes will be at that new valuation level—significant increases. Consider this part of your due diligence—and when it's unknown, we work with the county or may hire a real estate tax consultant to help us understand how the county will handle the taxes. That expense needs to be included in your assessment of the deal to determine if it's a doable thing for you.

ADVERTISING

Most facilities we have purchased have little to no advertising budget or they are using it in the wrong way—so make sure you calculate your expense pro formas with a reasonable advertising ratio. This depends on the facilities and the local market, but you need to create an online marketing budget. The cost of these are all over the board so you have to estimate it on a case by case basis. We utilize third-party service to help us with online advertising. You can get quotes from online advertising agencies to help you with this.

It's important to understand that every self storage operator does things a little bit differently and this affects the value of the facility. Determining the value of a location is a whole lot easier once you've managed a self storage facility for yourself, so you understand how to do it and where your expenses are.

Be aware of your own capabilities and what you can do and what you need to hire out. And you have to have a plan. Another facility may be making more money than you, but will they sustain that if the market turns? Your evaluation has to include a safety margin for that possibility. Your competitor could be hurt more than you in a market downturn because you have a plan.

REVENUE POTENTIAL

How many people are in that five-mile radius around the facility, do they own or rent, how many children do they have, and their income level are some of the big statistics that define how much the local customer base is willing to pay—along with the local competition. And because self storage is a supply-and-demand industry, you need to know how many SF of self storage competition is in that five-mile radius, what kinds of offerings they have, their occupancy rates, and what they charge.

> ## The local market determines the revenue potential.

A potential good deal with the kind of revenue potential you need will be charging less than market rates, underutilizing technology to reach customers, and leaving money on the table in other ways like poor collection processes. Red flags would be things like the competition is doing everything right but still has low occupancy—meaning the market may be saturated. I'll cover how to evaluate the competition and the deal in the next chapter.

Other macroeconomic factors like population trends in the area can be important to know too—if lots of people are moving into the area, that can be good and bad. It's good because there's more tenants coming in. It's bad because the population increase brings in other businesses to compete against you—possibly including the big boys in self storage, if the area will grow into a first-tier market anytime soon.

As you can see, the value is determined by the local environment. Saying it's a 5 cap doesn't tell you a thing about its potential or whether it's underperforming right now.

From an investor's perspective, the value in an asset is derived in just two ways:

- You can increase the return to shareholders.
- You can secure the return to shareholders.

What that means is you can either increase the return or make the return safer, more predictable. If revenues go up, that means it's worth more. Or if the odds of losing the revenue go down, that means it's worth more too—because now I know I'm going to get my money. That's how you need to look at it.

Understanding if you can increase revenues and how secure those revenues are comes down to how well you evaluate the supply and demand in the market, as well as the offerings you're bringing to the market.

MAKE SURE TO BUY THE ASSET ONLY

If you are inexperienced in the finance world, be careful to buy only assets—do not buy an LLC or S corporation that owns the asset. Keep what you buy separate from any organization so you are not taking on unknown liability.

HOW TO FIND DEALS

There are two kinds of deals:

1. Paid – You will pay top dollar for paid, on-market deals. I've never bought a deal on market. People who buy these deals many times are buying deals that others have turned down—they never see the ones I and others buy. If there's a "for sale" sign, it's not likely to be a good deal.

2. Earned – These are off-market deals and this is where the upside is. They also require more work and more know-how. You can also get off-market deals through a broker if they truly understand what you want, and you can still pay a broker to help you get off-market deals—and you should pay them. It's worth it to have a great relationship with a broker who is paid but will find deals for you before they ever go on the market. A broker who knows what they are doing and can bring you deal flow will pay dividends to you forever. They trust you, they know you will pay and they do less work and less headache for the buyer and it's done quick. It's the best situation for everyone involved. My portfolio is split 50-50 between off-market deals I've paid brokers to find and off-market deals I've found for myself.

Paid deals are always through broker relationships. Be very careful here because most brokers will either sell you a bad deal or won't understand what you want and won't give you what you want.

You need a broker who's on the same page as you. This requires working with them and educating them—and some just won't get it. But when you find one who understands what you want, they are worth a lot. I have benefited greatly from some good broker relationships.

Earned deals are the ones you find for yourself. Go to meetups, knock on doors, find them through banks, and find them through your market research. I have bought through banks more than once. Educate yourself and build your network and your team, and you'll be able to do this for yourself.

The majority of assets in the world are purchased through off-market deals. On-market deals are for retail investors. Off-market deals require more work and know-how, but are more profitable.

THE ACQUISITION FUNNEL

Earning the deal includes the entire process of finding your own deals. It's a lot of work because you need a funnel of information to identify a good deal. The facility, due diligence, negotiating the sale, and the purchase can be thought of as an *acquisition funnel,* where you start by casting a wide net, looking for the right market where you can compete, narrow your options to the facility in the right location with an owner who is interested in selling. If you find an opportunity in poorly managed operations, this may be the deal for you, when you can see money left on the table. In order to effectively negotiate with the owner/seller, you need to take their needs into account to come up with a price that makes you both happy and a purchase contract that results in the sale.

THE ACQUISITION FUNNEL

Identify a viable market

Identify all facilities in the market

Eliminate facilities that don't meet buying criteria
(Example: Approximately 60K-plus SF, on a
main road, with at least 10K traffic per day)
(includes site location)

Analyze the competition

Identify value-add opportunity

Collect potential seller contact info

Identify willing seller and analyze
their needs. Call, email, set
up meetings.

Identify the deal,
negotiate with
seller, get under
contract

Secure
financing

You've
got a
deal!

KEY TAKEAWAYS

▶ Understanding the value creators and value destroyers in self storage allows you to identify opportunities.

▶ Having a plan for how you will manage your facility helps you determine what your operating expenses will be.

▶ Your management plan will also be the basis for your cost estimate on capital expenditures.

CHAPTER 5

Financing Your Self Storage Facility

Money to buy, build, or convert to own self storage comes from two sources: yours or someone else's (OPM: other people's money). If you can self-fund the entire thing, you can sidestep a lot of work. The downside to that is you take on all the risk. It's most common to use your own money for the down payment (this can be up to 20% of the purchase price) and OPM for the rest.

I've said this before but it bears repeating: you need to know if you want this as a side thing or as your business. You can do either and that's one of the great things about it. But you need to know what you want and what you have to invest.

YOUR MONEY = DOWN PAYMENT

The down payment is usually your money—your starting capital. The down payment is also the equity you have in the deal. Also, to do a value-add strategy, you need to have more cash in hand than you may think you'll need. Improvements can cost a lot, depending on the facility and the market. You'll also need reserves for the unexpected.

For the rest of the purchase price, you can either self-fund or use OPM. Most people use OPM, but you need to be comfortable with that. If you're not, stick to smaller deals where you can entirely self-fund or find an owner-finance situation.

Let's say you have $100K, and you need $500K for the down payment. You ask somebody else for the difference because it's even better, less risky, when you get part of the down payment from other people. It's far easier to deal with other people than to deal with banks—they are horrible to deal with. It's much riskier to go to a bank. So it's an important step to figure out.

How you do the financing depends on how much capital you have and what you want to do. If you don't have the 20-30% down payment, you can get creative with someone else who has capital, and you give them a share of the equity in exchange.

To gain more perspective, join the community at SelfStorageIncome.com to engage and learn.

IF YOU WANT TO SELF-FUND HIGH GROWTH, MANAGE IT YOURSELF

We self-funded our deals starting out, and this is important because it depends on how you want to grow and what your strategy of growth is. If you want to grow fast, you want a portfolio, and you're self-funding (you're not syndicating), you need to get a big bang from your buck out of a storage facility. That's what I wanted, so I was buying deals and turning them around as fast as I could.

For example, I bought a facility for $3M and once the value and revenue of that facility came up (from my improvements and targeted marketing), it's estimated to be worth $6M. I'm going to either sell, collect revenue, or refinance to get my money out, and do it again. My goal in that case was to buy bigger and bigger—so I'm willing to sell the smaller one as a stepping-stone to what I really want.

That allows me to compound. It's the velocity of money—how quick that money changes hands and goes from asset to asset. So if you're self-funding, in my opinion it's really important that you're more hands-on—that you set up the systems and management yourself. That doesn't mean you're the one behind the desk every day, but if you are calling the shots, you'll learn how to add value and get a big return in a short period of time.

If you don't want to create a system for improving, for the value-add strategy, then you're not going to get the biggest return—but you will still get a great investment and diversification to your portfolio. So it's your choice.

BIGGER MARKET = MORE MONEY

This is obvious, but generally the bigger the market, the more money you need. In the smaller markets you may be able to self-fund or do seller financing. In a second-tier market, you're almost always self-funding plus OPM. In a first-tier market, you have to do 100% OPM. The point is that for those upper two tiers, you're probably never doing it on your own—it's too much money. It's $15-$20M.

One investor I know invests in third-tier, small markets with small facilities. He doesn't want to leave the small markets because he doesn't want to compete with the bigger players. He likes being forgotten. There are benefits to that. It's can be a great strategy—but you need to choose your market carefully to make sure it's a growing area and not shrinking, and another problem is you will never get a big uptick in appreciation. A facility purchased for $600K in northern Idaho will eventually be worth $1M, but it's going to be a long time. Again, choose the market that will help you reach your goals.

If you buy a $600K facility in the Boise area, you could probably make that $1M in six months. However, you have to know what you're doing in an overbuilt market like Boise to make that work. Smaller facilities like that still exist but it's not a place to learn the ropes.

GUARANTEED APPRECIATION

What we focus on is the *forced appreciation* or the *known upside,* and that's the upside I would call guaranteed—it's got nothing to do with typical inflation-driven market appreciation and is therefore much lower risk.

I look at the market and determine what the standard market rate is—let's say it's $1 per SF in revenue. That's where the good operators are. Then I find somebody who's a bad operator, and I see their revenue per SF is at $0.50. I know I can double my money because that higher rate is a known for that market.

A lot of people think about investing and they think the market's going to give them the appreciation. That can happen but that is pure speculation and that's not what we are showing you how to do—that's our number one rule: Do not count on market appreciation because that's out of your control. But that known, that guaranteed appreciation exists in the spread between the underperforming revenue and the standard revenue that's already in the market.

> # Do not count on market appreciation because that's out of your control.

I'm not guessing. I'm not thinking that customers will pay it. I know it. We have four facilities and they all receive these kinds of returns. We already know that people are currently willing to pay that rate. That's the market standard. That's where you get that jump, that spread; it's your magic number, so to speak. And it's all based on experience and researching the market.

WHERE TO START TO FINANCE YOUR BUSINESS

Some kinds of OPM are easier to work with than others. The banks are the worst, especially big banks. Friends and family can be one of the best ways to finance a purchase, but you need to know the legal language and set up a real agreement there, to reduce risk and preserve your relationships.

SOURCES OF OPM

Another source of OPM if you are in smaller markets can be seller financing. This is one of the great opportunities for purchasing individually owned facilities. This cuts out the middleman and can be set up to the benefit of both parties. I'll cover more on that below.

Banks

How you obtain financing for a self storage facility purchase is one of the biggest aspects of purchasing any real estate asset, and it is the reason most people fail. You need to get it right. At the time I am writing this book, there aren't a lot of financial players who understand how to underwrite self storage. My partner and I have had to educate them and show them the value and develop a relationship with them. The key is trust—show them you know what you are doing and understand the self storage industry.

All financiers are not created equal.

Finding the right financier takes time, and some will just not work out. You have to make your financier feel comfortable. If you are just starting out, you need to make a packet for the institution. List your partners and explain their expertise like a board—explain their experience and background. Show the bank how your team has expertise, even if it's really just you. You need to show them you aren't going to fail.

This is difficult. You will need a good financial partner unless you're going in with all cash. You need to find a good fit: someone who understands you and will go out to lunch and get a little bit past the professional relationship. They need to be comfortable with you and what you are doing.

You also have to trust the bank. There are certain banks I would never work with—such as the ones in the news that got caught out on something.

There are some avenues for working with brokers who specialize in self storage financing. Some banks specialize in self storage financing, but these tend to rigidly define the markets they will work in and typically those are first-tier markets with a lot of certainty built in.

Look at Smaller Banks or Credit Unions

Small community banks and credit unions are much more likely to work with you than large banks—local people you can see a future with. Larger banks are notoriously difficult to work with because of their rules and regulations. Sometimes you will hate the terms with a large bank.

We've worked successfully with credit unions. Boise is a fast-growing region with over a half a million people, but some of the big banks think we're still riding horses and hunting for our food. The local credit unions understand the value and the marketplace you are in. And you can meet the underwriter. Large banks have rules and you have to meet those rules or they say no.

There's massive value in developing a good relationship with a financial institution, too; you can find self storage assets that are in terrible financial situations (a balloon payment coming up, for example) that could be that value-add situation you are looking for.

Seller Financing

Seller financing is an excellent opportunity in the self storage industry because so many facilities are owned by individuals. This is especially likely for the smaller ones. When those owners decide they want to retire, they want to sell. They may say something like, "I'll sell it to you, you give me $200K, and I'll hold the note because I still want to make a monthly income from the payments."

To make this work, you need to know what they want from the deal. So seller financing is about relationships too, just like any other source of OPM—the seller needs to trust you and see you as someone who will make the payments as promised. Take the time to get to know them and show them you want to work with them.

Seller financing is usually a win-win situation with very little risk on either side. If you default, the seller gets the property back to sell again and typically keeps the down payment. There are a few things you need to know about setting up the agreement, but there will be no closing costs because it's just you and the seller—no middleman. This is one of the real leveraging opportunities in self storage. One of your primary goals is to keep your obligations on the note to a minimum. And, as I have mentioned, be certain that market is growing and not shrinking.

Be sure to include these details in the agreement you set up for seller financing:
- How much the down payment will be and the interest rate for the payments
- How interest is calculated
- Over how long a period the loan is amortized
- What the maturity date is
- What happens if you're late on a payment
- When the payment is due, and whether there is any grace period
- Which escrow company will be used
- How you legally notice the other party
- How insurance works
- No prepayment penalty (there might be a minimum number of years of payments)
- What to do if either party dies during the time frame of the agreement
- Exit strategy: include what happens if you default (a typical arrangement would be the property goes back to the seller and they keep the down payment)

WHAT ARE GOOD TERMS?

Here are the basics of what you need to look at:
1. Interest rate (depends on market conditions, LIBOR rates, and 10-year treasuries)
2. The legalese language that lenders can change, but you have to ask them (attorneys can help you there)
3. Amortization rates count a lot—you may want to consider lowering the amortization time frame because you'll pay less interest
4. Your exit strategy—it's important to know this and include the right terms so it can happen

This requires lots of work—you might go 90% of the way and realize it's not going to work. It's the same thing with the bankers. You need to have a relationship. There's currently a myth in the self storage industry that it's recession-*proof*—it can be but not in every case. Recession-resistant is a better term. It's not always going to be a home run. You have to do the work and have a plan.

KEY TAKEAWAYS

▶ Financing with OPM is about relationships and trust, no matter whose money it is—a bank's or your family's.

▶ If you are self-funding, you'll get the biggest return on your investment if you are involved in the management of the facility. This is a significant part of the value-add strategy.

▶ Seller (owner) financing can be a great option and a leverage opportunity in smaller markets.

CHAPTER 6

How to Evaluate the Competition and the Deal

Before you can evaluate a potential purchase, development, or conversion in self storage, you need to understand the local competition and the market. These things directly impact the revenue potential of that facility.

Nothing affects the rates you can charge more than the competition.

Self storage is more susceptible to supply and demand than apartment buildings, for instance, because of the month-to-month leases. And spring is the busy season for many markets.

Many facilities have their own style—a look or specialty, a niche. Competitor tracking will give you an idea of what your future may look like and where and how high you can move your rents. Look in a five-mile radius. "Secret shop" and go talk to owners and managers. You want to find out their occupancy rates and whether they have a waiting list or is everything available. If you find a lot of variability and a lot of competitors, this may not be a value-add opportunity and could put you at risk in a downturn.

Evaluating the competition is called *competitor tracking*. This is a data-driven set of activities to determine the competition in the local market you have chosen. Another way technology has changed the industry is the aggregation of data, which helps us make better decisions about the market. There are several information aggregator services that can help you develop storage facilities by showing you the current SF of self storage per capita that's on the market. This information is key in determining if the market you're considering is undersupplied or overbuilt. Use these kinds of tools and technology to collect this data and see what's going on in the local market now.

Understand that the data aggregation services are not always right, but they give you a good starting point. You still have to do your own groundwork and do your own online searches as if you were a customer. The data may show 30 SF per capita in this market and you're thinking, "Wow, that's nineteen feet overbuilt. I'm going to stay away from that."

Another aspect of competitor tracking you have to do yourself is looking at the online reviews for the competition's facilities. You need to see what people are saying about the facility and what kind of reputation they have. You also need to know if they're growing their online reviews or if that's static, meaning they're not putting a lot of effort into obtaining reviews—one more aspect of the online presence.

COMPETITOR ANALYSIS: WHAT TO TRACK

Make an Excel sheet with names, details about what they offer, their rates, specialties, and who is managing it (you need to know if they are a mom and pop versus a REIT-managed facility). Go to the city planning and zoning office and find out where new self storage facilities are being built. Find out where zoning for self storage is allowed. If there aren't any within five miles of you, that's a good sign. That reduces risk. Zoning can be changed, however, so it's not a guarantee.

Here's a basic list of what you need to look at:

- Ownership (and whether they are out of state or not)
- Management setup (third-party, on-site staff, etc.)
- Online presence
- Reviews
- Degree of automation
- Occupancy numbers
- Rates
- Curb appeal
- Number and type of units
  - Details on covered and not
  - Climate controlled or not
  - Unit lighting availability
  - Anything else you find
- Add-ons the competition is offering
  - Insurance
  - Boxes, pallets, etc.
- Meeting rooms and office space
- Security details

THE BIG PICTURE: HOW TO LOOK AT THE COMPETITION

What it comes down to is you're looking at how efficient the competitors are in the market and if they're capitalizing on the full potential. You need to understand, when you enter in the market, how you will be able to acquire and keep customers, offer better services, and run the facility better than the competitors in the market.

This is especially true when looking at the facility you're buying: you need to understand all the things they're doing wrong, how to turn those things around, what cost it will take to turn them around, and what revenue that will bring in. This is the basis of all underwriting: understanding competition and demand, identifying what that facility owner is doing wrong, the cost to change that, and the revenue those changes will create. Once you understand these things, you can understand where the opportunity lies.

FINDING FACILITIES THAT ARE LEAVING MONEY ON THE TABLE

We're looking for money left on the table: Money on the table is the difference between actual, collected rate revenue and the market rates plus additional lines of revenue or products not being offered—it's sitting there but they're not taking it. Money on the table does not mean future gains. It's the spread between what they're doing now and what they should be doing that is easily fixed. It doesn't mean you have to invest a ton of capital or change everything about the facility. It's simply operational-based differences that include rate management and product offerings, and it can be easily switched and turned around. See the case studies on Storage Investment #4 in chapters 6 and 7 for more on identifying money left on the table.

BEWARE THE BIG PLAYERS—BUT YOU CAN BENEFIT TOO

The big players can be great allies and there are good things that they do. But you have to understand how they operate. Some of the players come in and try to buy up all of the market at a discount, which can hurt you.

On average, REITs get higher dollars per SF per capita. Also, they invest in good markets—not all the time, but it can be a good sign of a good healthy market and also a sign of a higher SF per capita. So if REITs are in a market, it doesn't mean you shouldn't invest in it, but you have to analyze demand and your competitive ability even more.

It's important to look closely at who owns the competition and how they are managing it. This tells you a lot about what kind of competition they are. Especially for your first facility, beware of the big boys, the REIT-owned competition, but also know there are ways to be in the same market without competing head-to-head with them. There isn't a hard-and-fast rule about the population size or density in terms of where REITs will operate, and all is subject to change. The overall trend is that institutional ownership in self storage is increasing, and that consolidation isn't likely to change in the near future. In three to five years, the situation will look quite different than it does as of this writing.

One of the ways technology has changed the industry is enabling the people with the most data, the biggest budget, and the most access to technology to charge more and outperform others.

REITs have better data. Their revenue management system is better, they can find the best tenants, and they can pay more because all of the aggregated systems online, like Google and Facebook, are all bidding systems. So if you're blanket bidding, which means you'll just pay for anybody and you don't know who you're paying for (as compared to the person who knows exactly who they want), you may pay $1 per click while the bigger player knows they're a good customer so they will outbid you for that customer—they might pay $6. That's how pay per click works. And you'll never see that good customer.

Big players are also backing the disruptive technologies like Clutter and the on-demand storage facilities. However, they are playing in big cities and not in the one-off markets. We have one of these in Boise and while it's not catching on yet, it's an example of how markets can change and shows you why it's important to always have a plan and a safety margin. Property values across the country are rising and on-demand storage services may start taking a piece of the market in the future. On-demand storage is where they come to you, pick up your stuff, and take it to a location farther away. You have to be prepared for that possibility.

Look for high demand and competition that is mostly individuals—one-off owners—if possible. Also look for signs the market is growing, especially if it's a small market, to make sure demand will not erode from where it is now. And know that you can differentiate yourself through your offerings and cater to specific types of customers that the bigger competition may not be going after. The very localized self storage industry is all about supply and demand. And supply and demand are not all created equal. Supply is not just supply. The top quartile of supply will take up a huge percent of the customers because they're just better, and that's okay.

THE DANGER OF SMALL MARKETS

While small markets can be an opportunity, there is risk here too. The danger is that value can erode if it's an area that's shrinking in population. The value and revenues can erode away because the market's not growing. Worse, there's no one to buy your facility and you can be stuck. It can be a bad situation.

Once you get started and are making progress, consider joining a group like StoreLocal, which is a co-op of self storage owners who got together to increase their buying power so they can act more like the big boys. I am a member, and we can contract out to a third-party service and get lower rates because we're doing it as a group.

SELF STORAGE VALUE SPECIFICS

To recap, financing a self storage purchase involves knowledge about these things:
1. The potential value of the facility you want to buy (market analysis)
2. The current value of the facility you want to buy (data from owner plus your own analysis)
3. An estimate of the cost of upgrades plus more for the unexpected
4. The cost of borrowing money and who you will get it from

The previous section covered how to research the local market where you want to buy. It involves these activities:
- Evaluating the competition
- Identifying who the competition's customers are (price conscious, location conscious, or quality conscious)
- Knowing the demand for self storage (occupancy rates plus local population of your target customer)
- Knowing current rates in the area

This is what helps you estimate the revenue potential of a given facility. If it's an overbuilt market but an underperforming facility, would it still be profitable if you had to lower rates or couldn't reach full occupancy? If you can't build in a safety margin, this may not be the opportunity you thought it was.

After your research, you will know if the current tenants are mostly price-conscious by the rates being charged and the outward appearance and condition of the facility. This alone can be enough upside to make it a viable value-add opportunity—especially if the competition is not focused on this kind of customer.

DETERMINING VALUE: USE YOUR OWN NUMBERS

Determining the value of a facility is about understanding for yourself what the potential of a property is. You can't use the numbers anyone else provides because their expense ratio, type of customer, and revenue per SF will be different than yours—unless they are already doing everything right, as you intend to do it.

> You need to understand what kind of customer the facility is currently serving, how to identify money that's being left on the table by the current operator, and what your own expense ratio will be for the way you plan to operate the business.

These details should be sounding familiar, but they are worth repeating. This is the "secret sauce" to my value-add strategy.

Things to Know About Management for Maximizing Revenue

Revenue management is one of the major determinations of a successful facility versus a facility that has little growth. Revenue management is more than just adding on more products and offerings and raising your street rates. *Street rates* are what is being offered as a new customer comes in. Actual rates are the rates people are receiving within the facility. This is key and important to understand. When evaluating markets, you may be looking at the street rates and they look really high. Then you find out they weren't doing active revenue management and weren't actively increasing their rates. So 50% of the facility was being charged half of the street rate. This is money on the table—but you wouldn't know it until you dig into the books. Often what's actually being charged is vastly different from the street rate.

With revenue management, dynamic pricing is key. We have an aggressive rate increase and pricing structure at all our facilities. Most of the facilities we buy have a static rate increase or a uniform rate increase process. That means all of their 10 x 10s are one price. All of their 20 x 20s are another price. They price by unit size. Our pricing is determined on a few factors: local market supply and demand, our facility's supply and demand, and timing.

In our markets, we are almost always the price leader. Not only are we the price leader but at our stabilized facilities, none of our tenants go more than six to nine months without receiving a rate increase. At our facilities that have higher demand, they receive larger rate increases. At our facilities that have more vacancies, they receive lower rate increases. But they all receive individual rate increases based upon when they arrived in the facility. The net effect is that in any given week, multiple people in our facility are getting rate increases. So the revenue is continually trending up because every individual is getting rate increases, every six to nine months from when they signed up. This is important because it creates dynamic revenue flow and increase and allows us to systematically increase our street rate.

Again—the difference between the street rate and what is actually being charged, plus insurance fees, better management of bad debt, and additional product revenue is what we call money left on the table—and you can recover that money immediately through bumps in operational practices.

There are lots of different products in terms of sizes and types of self storage units, and finding value can be in the details. Look beyond the average price per SF to see what each unit size is renting for and which sizes are in demand. See more details under Maximizing Revenue in the operations chapter.

Additional Product Lines

Add-on products can have a significant impact on your revenue growth. Self storage is about more than the unit itself—and you can set up your management policies to your own benefit. All of our facilities require insurance or pro-tection plans for all units—it's our policy and results in the majority of tenants purchasing our insurance. Other products offer the customer convenience and ways to protect their belongings, like boxes, bed covers, and crates and pallets to keep things off the floor.

Have you ever been online and purchased a product and, as you are check-ing out, you are offered an add-on product or a discount or a way to bundle and save? What that online store is trying to do is increase your total cart's value. So by the time you check out, you were upsold and your cart now has risen in price. In storage, it's the same thing. A customer comes in to rent a 10 x 10 and we'll have them buy insurance and rent crates to set their things on and bed covers, etc. We upsell them into a climate-controlled unit or even sell them more than one unit.

By the time they leave, their cart value is higher than originally planned. We want that customer to have a higher cart. That's the frontline revenue manage-ment, which is a focus on sales and increasing the cart's size. Back-end revenue management is rate management and aggressive rate increase schedules, and as you can see from our Storage Investment #1 example later in this chapter, it makes a huge difference.

Rate Comparisons to Maximize price per SF

Just because a location has a $0.60 per SF revenue doesn't mean all the units are maximized. In "mom and pop" dominated areas, there can be a massive variance in price per SF. That's because they priced it on a price point and not a price per SF. So the 10 x 20 is less per SF than the smaller ones, and that doesn't make sense in real estate. Those rates should be increased. Take the square foot-age and look at revenue prices and look at what it's worth. You want all of the SF to earn the same or close.

Do a comparison—where are the street rates and where are the actual rates? Sometimes people don't raise the rates and some people are paying half the street rates. This is common knowledge with the big storage players.

STATIC RATE INCREASES VERSUS DYNAMIC RATE INCREASES: AN EXAMPLE

Let me show you the difference over a three-year period of static rate increases versus active rate increase revenue management. Our Storage Investment #1 had virtually no increases before we purchased it and three years later, its performance had changed dramatically by focusing purely on revenue management. We did not upgrade the facility or anything else.

Snapshot of Investment #1 before we acquired the facility:

2013	2012	2011
Gross Revenue: $280,662	Gross Revenue: $282,524	Gross Revenue: $280,379
Cap Rate: 6.5%	Cap Rate: 6.8%	Cap Rate: 6.3%

Snapshot after we acquired the facility:

2016	2015	2014
Gross Revenue: $421,789	Gross Revenue: $370,011	Gross Revenue: $322,453
Cap Rate: 11.4%	Cap Rate: 10.6%	Cap Rate: 8.5%
Added Equity: $847,819	Added Equity: $711,853	Added Equity: $647,780

The facility was purchased for $2,141,000 for a 6.5% capitalization rate in 2013. Three years later, the facility had added $1,607,452 in value at that 6.5% capitalization rate. We put $762,350 down on the property and gained that back in the first year and a half. By year three, we were at a 32% cash on cash return.

THE IMPACT OF CAPITAL IMPROVEMENTS

How you intend to improve the facility also impacts the potential value and revenue. If the facility you want to buy has a low occupancy rate in 5 x 10 units and is 100% occupied in 10 x 10s and 10 x 20s with a waiting list, is it possible to renovate to convert those small units into larger ones?

We did that for a huge revenue increase at our Storage Investment #2 facility. Here are the numbers:

Size	Pre-acquisition Rate	Post-acquisition Rate
5 x 10	$50	$58
10 x 10	$78	$87
10 x 20	$120	$156

If the current management is using a low-tech PMS and you plan to upgrade that so a single on-site employee is all that is needed, your expense ratio will be different. Your PMS should interface with some of the capital improvements you make, like gate access.

Also be aware of common "gotchas" (I'm calling them potholes) described below.

POTHOLES TO AVOID

There are a few things to watch out for when you are evaluating a potential purchase.

Ask About Vendors: When you are exploring the opportunity, ask for information about all the third-party vendors the seller is using. Most of the time you will not be using their vendors but knowing which vendors they are using and for what services helps you see where the performance problems are and where expenses are. Negotiating the purchase also requires figuring out if you will be continuing with any of the current vendors or assuming any long-term vendor contracts.

We recommend against carrying over existing vendors in general—your management methods will be different and it's best to start fresh and keep contracts short term.

As an example, at the Storage Investment #1, the seller had signed a three-year contract with Yellow Pages advertising of $10,000 per year. We do not use Yellow Pages advertising—no one does.

Advertising expense: Sometimes the advertising expenses are left off the books, so ask about it specifically if you don't see it.

Owner/managers: Many mom and pop owner/managers do all the work themselves and do not include an accounting of their time in the expenses provided for the sale. Or they simply fail to include management fees in the accounting. So you must ask the owner of any self storage facility, where the owner is the manager, for a reckoning of their time spent as the manager, any management fees, and also their time spent in any other role. When that information is missing, it can have a huge impact on the expense ratio. It can make the difference between a profit and a loss. It's important to know who is managing it and how it's being managed so you have a true understanding of what you're buying and how the expenses look.

Property tax increase with improved valuation: This is another critical one. You need to understand how property taxes work in the local county where you are buying. If you buy an underperforming and undervalued facility, improve it, and double the revenue, the property taxes will go up substantially. You need to take that into account in your accounting of the expense ratio for the facility—don't be surprised by this. You should be able to estimate what they will be, based on the current property tax bill.

Mom and pop facilities in particular can be a surprise. If, 30 yours ago, they built the facility for $1M and you're buying it for $5M, the taxes will be at the $5M rate. You have to understand what this will cost you before you buy—you have to underwrite it for that new property cost.

For example, at Storage Investment #3, the property taxes were averaging $55,000 per year. After several years of improving the business, the property taxes ballooned to $150,000 per year. Property taxes can kill your investment if you don't account for them in the beginning.

HOW TO DECIDE TO BUY OR NOT TO BUY

Break down your decision-making process into two simple parts: Look at what's in your control and what's not. Two critical things are not in your control: supply and demand; and the facility's location and the local economics.

1. WHAT'S NOT IN YOUR CONTROL

Supply and demand

This is the most underappreciated thing about the evaluation. Most people we talk about are still building storage with an attitude of "build it, and they will come."

What is the optimum SF per capita in this market? They don't know. And they don't know the current SF per capita.

It's important to understand that it's a hyper-localized market. There are areas that are super-saturated, but 30 minutes away is a huge opportunity. A lot of people have rules about this—such as 8 SF per capita means there's too much. However, I am in markets that have 15 SF per capita.

Also, what's more concerning is what's coming in the pipeline. You need to know the term "zombie supply." Zombie supply is unknown supply—as to quality and specialties and the resulting demand for that. You can't assume that everyone building has done an analysis and knows whether there is demand to meet the new supply they are bringing on the market. I am more scared of this than the current situation. Permits have been signed, banks are ready to go, and we go into a recession. We're seeing this now, at the time of this writing. Over the past two years, massive developments have been underway in many markets. We're in a recession and new facilities can't get tenants so they lower prices. The whole market ends up lowering prices to compete over a small number of consumers because demand has dropped. Do they stop building? No. And when that comes on the market, in the middle of a recession, it can make unexpected dynamics. There's a lag, a tail, to development, which can't be stopped. If you're developing and a year later when you open your doors, you're in a recession, you can't take it back. And that just adds to the vacancy problem.

You need to work with local city and county government, so you know what's coming in the pipeline.

Zombie supply rises from the dead and comes and kills you. You don't see it. It's driven by REITs. When they report their occupancy, they don't include what's coming or not filled—what they call unstabilized assets.

There are three main online data aggregator services. Using one of these, in our local market, we can take what the city tells us and still find something being built that no one knew about. Also make sure you know all the light industrial zoned areas around.

Location and Economics

You can't change location. Easy access is important, not near other facilities. Dive into your consumer's perspective and their experience with the facility.

At some point, self storage is a type of commodity. You cannot fight against 3M SF already on the market. There are things you can do to mitigate it, but prices are going to drop. You want to be the best in the pack and lead ahead.

We will not go on to part 2 of the process (what's in your control) if we can't meet our requirements in part 1. You can be lucky, and this happens all the time—part 1 was good but we didn't know it and went ahead with the project and it all worked. But this isn't the 90s or just after 2008 anymore.

2. WHAT'S IN YOUR CONTROL

Once you've eliminated those projects with deal-killer things that are out of your control, start looking at what's in your control. I am a huge proponent of the value-add method of buying—buy it and turn it around. Focus on quality aspects that are missing and that you can fix—so you need to find those facilities that could be improved in the quality.

If we are in an area with lots of demand and a good location and the facility is a piece of junk, I'm buying it. That's my buy signal. I know that most of their tenants are there for the low price.

Customer Experience

Your management and how you renovate the facility directly impact the customer experience—how it looks and how it makes them feel. This includes having a brand strategy that presents a consistent, connected appearance online, in the showroom, and in your staff. The manager should have a branded uniform and be trained in the art of customer service and sales.

When we think about quality, we look at the experience of the tenant as they come in. Part of the customer's experience is the impact your brand makes—and you are making an impact, whether you have a plan or not. Make it a good one. The customer's experience is part of that branding.

The facility has to have curb appeal and a nice appearance. This creates perceived value, physically from the street and also online—the website.

The showroom should be open with multiple offerings. We usually will gut the entire showroom and create a franchise look. We build a completely new office and have added climate-controlled units in an area that was being used for open parking—because we can charge much higher rates for those than open parking. We will usually leave covered parking but could get a lot better rates from other types of units than open parking. We pave it if it's not already paved. These are the basic things we always do. We figured out what works and then reproduced that office design in other locations. The result is people feel safe and that we will protect their belongings.

Quality and offering of the actual units: This one alone can be your value add if they are done wrong. For example, we bought a facility that had over 300 5 x 5 units. The 5 x 5 units were only 30% occupied and the place was failing. It was under 60% occupied in total. We changed the offering by changing the appearance and the unit sizes based on the demand that was in the market. The way it was built made this renovation easy and that was attractive to us.

That facility was charging $0.26 per SF and was 60% occupied. We brought it up to $0.60 per SF and over 90% occupied. They had simply gotten the demand for unit sizes wrong. Customers didn't want 5 x 5s.

Again, here's what we do:

- Curbside appeal
- Quality and security
- Branding
- Showroom
- Offering: what kind of units plus add-on products
- Revenue management and pricing

We usually add technologies for automation and wine storage or other climate control; we make rows wider so semis can get through so it will be accessible for businesses.

Stabilizing Cash Flow

Part of your management plan should include stabilizing cash flows through how you execute: adding on superior service, brand recognition, ease of use, and ancillary products and services. Combined with an aggressive and effective marketing system, you can stabilize the cash flows while continuing to grow them in the future. That's the only thing that will give you long-term value and revenue.

This also includes other aspects of operations and management that you can do better. It's the accumulation of how you structure the offerings. This combines the online strategy with your groundwork strategy. (It's simple, but you need to keep the facility clean.) And here's what's not discussed: marketing strategy. You need to find those tenants who are focused on quality and get them in your showroom.

One expense category that can be overlooked is how your management handles delinquencies and bad debts. Your policies and practices can bring these losses down from 10% to 3%. This includes vacant units that weren't on the market because things moved too slowly when handling those delinquencies.

Check out my blogs on SelfStorageIncome.com and my YouTube videos for more examples and discussion on evaluating a deal and what makes a great opportunity. The case study at the end of this chapter also shows step by step considerations to help you see how this is done.

DEAL EVALUATION IS A PYRAMID WITH FOUR LAYERS

Here's a concept that helps you to see the importance and priority of the deal evaluation process.

1. Supply and demand is the base.
2. Location and local economics is the next layer.
3. Third is quality and offerings.
4. The pinnacle is operations—the management of your facility.

The bottom two layers are things you cannot change and must be in your favor from the beginning or you don't go. The top two layers are the things you can change, and this is where you can identify an opportunity, where there might be money on the table. If those two things are already top-notch, there's probably no upside and no opportunity. Without the management done right, you won't get what you want out of a facility. Sometimes that's the only thing we need to upgrade, even to facilities that are beautiful and don't require any improvements.

The four layers of the deal evaluation pyramid.

NEGOTIATING WITH THE SELLER

As an example of how to negotiate with the seller, I recently helped someone buy a small facility. The owners were having a hard time getting accurate records so the buyer could obtain financing. The buyer was getting frustrated and the bank was frustrated. We went to the owners and worked with them to do owner financing and made the contract non-recourse—so if any of their information provided was wrong, the contract could be readjusted.

Make sure to check for the gotchas, the potholes I described earlier in this chapter—expenses that are often overlooked. Have an honest conversation about the true expenses and how they use that to calculate the sale price.

For sellers, it's not always about the highest price. If you can take care of their needs and wants, you can often get deals done that ordinarily couldn't get it done. Find a way to set it up so it's a win for everyone.

NEGOTIATION DEAL-BREAKERS

Deal-breakers include unreasonable requests or not waiving liability. Often, deal-breakers come in the contract. You don't want to catch a falling knife or a bagful of liability. That's why you want to structure the deal with the asset purchase only. If something is set up as an S corporation, you may be asked to buy the S corp—but those are structured with shares and may have liabilities you don't even know about. Don't buy that—you want the business organization to stay with the seller and buy the asset itself from the S corp (for instance), but not the S corp itself. So have your attorney *and* accountant evaluate all deals you are considering.

> # Most deal-breaker details surface in conversations with attorneys and accountants.

All deals should be reviewed by them, and make sure you listen to them.

If you start to feel the seller isn't being honest or might be hiding something, that's a big red flag. We looked at a deal once that was built on a lumber mill site. We noticed a water drainage going into a hole that had no exit, and asked about it. We wondered if it could be going into a pile of sawdust that could be part of the foundation. We asked the seller to have it examined. The seller refused to do this because if he did, he would have had to publish the results to all buyers. That was a deal-breaker—and we walked away.

CASE STUDY: STORAGE INVESTMENT #4 PART I

Let's say you have identified a third-tier market that is not overbuilt. You have a good sense of the top end that you can charge for rates, based on data for the area plus the judgment you've developed from research online and in other areas. You've got your eye on a couple of locations that seem to be charging less than the market rate and they don't have the curb appeal of the others.

An example is our Storage Investment #4 that we purchased. An appraiser had valued the asset at $3M. Few appraisers know how to value self storage based on its revenue potential—and we knew better than to take that appraisal at face value. After competing with several national brands who kept driving the price up, we came back and offered to pay $4.8M for the property with $1.2M down. Everyone thought we overpaid (it was a 5 cap).

We were right. The turnaround details on this facility are described in Part II of this case study at the end of the next chapter.

We knew the property was undervalued, and not just because the appraiser was wrong. Significant revenue was being left on the table because of the way it was managed. The appearance of the facility and the below-market rates they were charging were attracting price-conscious customers only. They had no online presence. The units were 100% occupied, but about 10% of those weren't paying and weren't being collected on or evicted. In that performance snapshot, we knew we could probably more than double the revenue with a facelift, technology upgrades, and rate increases that only the quality-conscious tenants would pay. And we knew those quality-conscious tenants were close by.

You have to make your own evaluation and determine what the potential revenue of a facility would be if you were running it. How do you go about evaluating the facilities you find to identify a deal that meets your objectives?

Here is the deal evaluation pyramid broken out into questions for you to answer with some basics for what you need to look for:

Question 1: Is it a good location? Location is the one thing you can't fix so it has to be right, no matter what else is wrong. A good location is close to potential tenants and is easy to access. It's also a benefit if there isn't another self storage facility a block away. High traffic is a main goal, but ease of entrance and exit can be a major issue for you and your customers. Make sure the driveways and parking can accommodate incoming and outgoing traffic, or can be easily upgraded to accomplish that.

For Storage Investment #4, it was a good location with lots of traffic and nearby subdivisions.

Question 2: What's the curb appeal? You want poor curb appeal that can be fixed with a little capital expenditure. This is an important component of the value-add strategy.

The Storage Investment #4 location was run down. Nothing had been done to it in years.

Question 3: Who and where is the owner? What you want is an individual who has only one location, possibly two. Ideally that owner lives out of state, doesn't visit the facility, and hasn't seen it in years. However, smaller facilities may have an on-site owner/manager and that isn't a dealbreaker. You need to get to know them and what they want. They may be open to owner financing, which can be a great leverage point for you and provide the passive income they may need.

The Storage Investment #4 location was being run by the state. In order to not appear to be competing against local businesses, the management was charging below market rates and doing very little to maintain it.

Question 4: Is it 90%-plus occupied? Ideally this is a yes. However if it's a no, there may be a fixable reason for that. Find out what types of units are vacant. If the vacancies are all 5 x 5 units, and all the 10 x 10s and 10 x 20s are full, it's clear that nobody wants those small units. So a "No, but it's fixable" answer could be a real opportunity, if you can renovate to offer a better mix of unit sizes.

For Storage Investment #4, it was 100% occupied but not all tenants were paying. So the economic occupancy was more like 85% because of nonpayment and bad debts.

Question 5: What kind of tenants is it serving? These are the three kinds of tenants: price conscious, location conscious, and quality conscious. You want to purchase a facility that serves price-conscious tenants and upgrade it and the rates so the price-conscious tenants leave, and then you can fill it up with quality-conscious tenants at a higher price.

Question 6: Are the rates below market? You want this to be a yes too. You need some upside room to increase rates.

The Storage Investment #4 facility's rates were below market at the time we purchased it.

Question 7: How is revenue management being handled? If they don't charge late fees, don't have a good collections process in place or a vendor who handles that for them, and are slow to conduct auctions on abandoned units, they are leaving money on the table. If they don't have any add-on products such as insurance, boxes, bed sheets, and pallets, they are leaving money on the table.

The #4 facility's management was leaving significant money on the table.

Question 8: What is your value proposition? You have to have a plan that you use to calculate the potential revenue, so you can include the costs of any improvements and upgrades. The plan needs to include what type of unit upgrades you are going to make, what rates you can charge once it's upgraded, and the cost of your marketing strategy. It should also include a safety margin in case the market drops and you can't fill all your units or you have to lower your prices.

Our plan for the #4 location was to give the facility a facelift, update the showroom, and raise rates to drive out the price-conscious customers. See the results of our efforts in Case Study: Storage Investment #4 Part II in the next chapter.

KEY TAKEAWAYS

▶ You have to research the market, no matter how you intend to enter it. Every analysis has to include knowledge about local supply and demand, current rates, how the facilities are being marketed, and who owns them.

▶ The value of a facility is based on its local market.

▶ Always have a value proposition and calculate your projected revenue and value increases before you buy, build, or convert.

CHAPTER 7

Self Storage Operations: Turning Around a Self Storage Facility

Now that you understand what creates value and what affects risk, we can address what to do when you have just purchased an underperforming facility and how to turn it around. Here's what we do: Understand what the market needs and provide it; upgrade curbside appeal, quality, security, branding, and showroom; customize and reprice offerings, including what kind of units; manage revenue with effective staff training and hiring practices; and market the facility with an effective online strategy.

This chapter contains critical information about self storage business operations that you need in order to not only run your first facility but know what to look for when you are choosing what to buy or build. As a start, knowing what has to happen on "transfer" or "changing" day will help you know how to negotiate a purchase and help you understand how all the pieces of operation tie together.

The rest of the chapter includes information you will need to have considered and decided how you intend to proceed before you get to changing day—it's what you need to know to prepare for changing day.

Let's suppose you've found the facility you want to buy, made the deal, and you're about to take possession.

TRANSFER DAY (OR CHANGING DAY)

Transfer day is the day of ownership transition. I include this here because some of what happens here is negotiated with the sale, and also you need to plan for this day so there are no surprises. A good broker and title company will help. One of the simple things you need to do is transfer the utilities to your name. Most of the other things need to be negotiated.

The beautiful thing about real estate is it's been around forever, so the laws are very mainstream and very rigid. That's nice because the title transfer process is easy as a result.

During the sale negotiation, there are many decisions to work out concerning who's going to pay for what and for how long.

We've had deals where we took over a facility on the 15th of the month but decided to prorate everything to the beginning of that month (two weeks earlier) or to the end—the beginning of the next month. These details all need to be figured out and included in the agreement. The title officer will ask about prorations. It can get very granular, and not in a good way. We've had facilities where we had to do these prorations unit by unit—and it can be a long night.

VENDOR CONTRACT TRANSITIONS

Concerning vendors, you also have to decide who's going to pay for what contract and what's going to continue. We've had situations where we were not going to assume a contract for a vendor relationship.

This is about looking carefully at your expenses and how you are going to run the facility. You may plan to operate differently and don't need that service. It's not just the price tag—look at the contract that owner had with that vendor. If they have a deal that will last for 10 years and the price will grow 10% per year, what happens? Is the seller going to take that on or subtract that from the purchase price? You don't want to take that on. You need to know these details before you take over, and how things like that will happen. If you don't explore all those details, you'll have some *really* long nights on transfer days because you're finding out things you never wanted to find out. We've had vendors show up months after transfer day, asking us why they haven't been paid.

In general, we recommend not continuing existing vendor relationships. It's always better to negotiate your own deals. And don't do long-term contracts in general, even if you have to pay a higher price. The self storage industry is changing quickly. You do not want to be stuck in long-term contracts with vendors who are being bought constantly, not to mention technology changes can happen that make them irrelevant. They will hold you to that contract. You need to be able to move and adapt your operations in short time frames. We recommend a maximum of a year contract and that's only on year one—after that, go to a 30-day notification to end the contract. If you do more than that, you will find yourself tied for sure.

COMMON VENDOR CONTRACTED SERVICES

- Landscaping
- Snow removal
- Maintenance contractor
- Cell towers
- Advertising and marketing
- Software management
- IT assistance
- Ground leases other than storage

PERSONNEL TRANSITIONS

You need to make sure the existing personnel are either on- or off-board, and you need to have someone ready to step in if they are off—whether it's you or someone else. For your first purchase, you need to be in on it. Even if you have a manager, you need to be involved because you will learn so much about the industry and whether you are getting value from this person and their service.

With most of our facilities, when we bought the facility, the existing manager did not stay on board. We were buying underperforming facilities, and usually that manager was a big part of that poor performance. They had 100%

power and say as to what was happening. And in some cases, they took advantage of the situation.

If you are keeping the current manager, you need to make sure to clearly define your way of running your facility. Don't assume because they have been managing the property that they know how *you* want things done. They should be treated as though they are a new hire when it comes to policies, standards, and procedures.

Our facilities are very structured, and we want all personnel to follow policies and procedures. We need a professional manager who has been trained in our way of doing business. What we have seen is that often the management changes were too drastic compared to the previous management policies, and existing managers could not meet our expectations. So it's important to make sure the manager you hire will be a good fit and will be able to perform as needed. This can be a lot to ask of someone, and you may need a backup manager in case the first one can't do it. Many times, the original manager doesn't work out.

LOGISTICS

See the Changing Day Checklist for more details, but one thing you should find out before changing day is whether the previous owner had mail delivered to the on-site physical location or to a post office box. You will need to transfer the box to the new owner if there is one.

CHANGING DAY CHECKLIST

Now that you have the keys, a lot of things need to happen at the same time. Branding and marketing strategy are tied in with facility upgrades, and those upgrades need to start soon, but you need to tie everything together—how much automation you want to have is tied to the property management systems (PMS) software you buy and your website ties into that.

The capabilities of the PMS directly impact online payment and sales of units and ancillary products and how sophisticated your marketing strategies can be. Curb appeal and landscaping tie into branding, as does the website and showroom design and features. Updates and customization of sizes and types of storage units are also tied into your branding. Step one is to read this entire chapter before making a move, so you have an understanding of how your big picture strategy needs to work.

What follows is a basic changing day checklist. Every facility will have special details, but this will get you started with the common things you need to do.

☐ 1. Onboard new employee(s).

☐ 2. Start training process for new employee(s).

☐ 3. Establish till.

☐ 4. Establish banking.

☐ 5. Ensure that all items in property list (regarding office, resale merchandise, and maintenance items) match what can be found on property.

    a. Do a supply run for any remaining needed items

☐ 6. If retaining employee, ask employee if there are any known maintenance issues.

☐ 7. Familiarize yourself with existing filing system.

☐ 8. Perform **lock audit:**

    a. Ensure that all units that Property Management System (PMS) says are vacant are vacant and ready to rent

    b. Ensure that all units that PMS says are occupied and non-delinquent have tenant locks on them

    c. Ensure that all units that PMS says are severely delinquent are over-locked (in accordance with state regulations/timeframes)

☐ 9. Have facility re-keyed.

☐ 10. Audit files (look for discrepancies in paperwork, leases that might be missing, etc.).

☐ 11. Take inventory of any existing company vendors in operation under old management. If you intend to continue using them, change transfer the account information into your name. Examples may include:

    a. Security cameras/monitoring programs

    b. Alarm systems

    c. Power company

    d. Waste management company

e. Water

f. Sprinkler care/lawncare

g. Snow plowing

h. Facility maintenance

i. Door repair

j. Property management system

k. Gate management system

l. Merchandise for sale

m. Mailbox

n. Janitorial services

o. Website management

p. Phone system

q. Advertising company

r. Portable restroom services

s. Etc.

☐ 12. Implement desired software programs (if changing).

    a. If changing PMS from one to another:

        i. Make sure that gate system is compatible with desired PMS

        ii. Before switching, print notes and ledger for every tenant, print any reports regarding autopay information, rent roll, account paid-through dates, current balances, and any other operational/accounting reports containing information you will need after transfer is complete

        iii. Contact desired PMS to transfer data from existing PMS system

        iv. Compare information reports from old PMS to current information listed in new PMS and ensure they match (and make any corrections needed)

☐ 13. Identify how many accounts are missing information.

    a. Phone numbers

    b. Addresses

    c. Email addresses

☐ 14. Send out announcement of new ownership notices (include new/changing rules and regulations, and a copy of your contract for tenants to sign).

☐ 15. Considering units that are severely delinquent:

    a. Identify where the units/accounts are in the lien/auction process, and prepare to take the next step

☐ 16. Change signage over to new facility.

    a. Look for signage that states hours of operation

    b. Remove signage in office containing outdated information/policies

☐ 17. Change website (and internet sites where you are listed) to your company's information and pricing.

☐ 18. Clean and assess office needs.

☐ 19. Assess existing equipment (printers/computers/monitors, etc.) and replace if necessary.

WHAT YOU NEED TO KNOW ABOUT OPERATING A SELF STORAGE FACILITY

Your first decision (and you should know the answer to this before you buy) is to determine how will it be managed.

TWO TYPES OF MANAGEMENT

You should make the decision about how you want to manage the facility before you purchase it. Here's some information to help you evaluate management.

Self-Management

Knowing you want to manage a self storage facility yourself helps you choose the right kind of facility to purchase. How big a facility you buy is dictated by how many employees you are willing to hire and their roles. While going small may seem like a safe approach, the margins are unforgiving in small facilities and you may be better off looking at a midsized facility—or else be sure the expenses will not increase dramatically due to one or more of the potholes I described.

For flipping a facility and a value-add strategy to create wealth, self-managing is the way to go. And by this I don't mean you're the one on-site every day, although you can do that too. You find third-party vendors, the right PMS, and get the systems set up with trained employees, and then you can walk away.

For smaller facilities and the smaller markets in about three-quarters of the U.S., REITs won't even operate. So you won't have the option of hiring a REIT-operated management company, although you may find a midsize management company. Not all midsize companies know what they are doing; we hired one and they nearly ran our facility into the ground. We did a better job of managing the facility ourselves, even when we didn't know what we were doing. So keep an eye on any management company you hire.

Self-management is not always the best route to take—you need to know when to hire help as it is very technical and there are a lot of ins and outs that can have a big impact on revenue. So evaluate your willingness to learn and where you will need to bring in help. My self storage course "Creating Wealth and Income Through Self Storage" on Teachable and SelfStorageIncome.com is designed for those who want to self-manage a facility, and much of that content is here in this book. The Self Storage Income Facebook and Instagram groups are great places to learn how others are doing things, so join those groups to get in on the discussions.

Third-Party Management

There are more options now than ever before with third-party management of self storage businesses. What you want to avoid is a company that specializes in apartments and has no real understanding of self storage. It is a completely different business model. In fact, finding out that a facility is being managed by a third party without specialization in self storage is a great way to find potential investment opportunities: chances are they are not run well. Avoid them for your own facility at all costs.

Third-party management companies come in essentially three types:
- Individual operators who run their own facility and also manage other facilities

- Midsize regional management companies that specialize in self storage or a larger single operator
- REIT-owned, national management companies

No matter what kind you are choosing, ask questions. Some of them still act like it's the 80s and have a very passive management style. That's not what you want. Ask them how they have implemented technology, optimized the online space, and utilized mobile-friendly technologies. Ask how they rank and how they end up at the top of the search engines. Ask how to get out of the contract. Some of the fees may be standing and some are negotiable. Options include a flat fee based on revenue, a sign-on fee, and some will want to be bonused or allowed to charge higher fees based on performance.

So ask all kinds of questions and they should expect that. Ask for case studies—when they've turned around a failing facility and what they've done when there's too much competition—to see how they deal with these issues. How do they beat the competition? You want a very active, tech approach to everything. They should understand the industry and the nuances that make a difference.

Each type of management has pros and cons. Your best value can come from the individual operators, although you need to vet them carefully. Research the facilities they already operate as if you were going to buy it. Are they doing the right things? If not, you may be better off paying a bit more.

The midsize operators will typically still have reasonable rates and a hands-on feel to the service. You will likely have some input into how it's run. Vet them carefully, asking about the types of facilities they run and their philosophy of management. If none of their facilities are like yours, they may not be a good fit. You want direct experience with the same offerings your facility has. You may not always know what you're getting.

The big, REIT-owned national companies have a safety-net feeling, whether it's real or not. They have brand-name recognition and will project an image that they follow best practices in the industry. Again, ask to see the asset types they manage to make sure they will know how to work with yours.

REITs will have higher fees, usually around 6% of gross margin, and you will have no say in how it's managed. Plus, they keep all add-on services for themselves and that is a lot of revenue. It's also not easy to get out of their contracts—there may be fees associated with exiting. They will treat your tenants similarly: it will be difficult for tenants to get out of their contracts.

PROPERTY MANAGEMENT SYSTEMS: A CRITICAL DECISION

You need a PMS (property management system) to streamline daily operations. This one decision can have a significant impact on your expense ratio, so research it well before choosing one.

What you want is a software system that has an "open" API—application programming interface—to allow sharing of data for marketing, occupancy, inventory, and revenue analysis. You can hire third-party specialists to plug in and operate your business, if your management software allows it. Some software packages can take care of signing leases, setting up autopayments, renewals, gate access, and more. One of our facilities is completely automated in this way.

Look for a package that has both cloud and "on premise" deployments, if you want to maximize automation of your facility.

It's important to ask a lot of questions and look closely at any contract you will sign for a PMS. What happens when we break up? Do I get my data? How will that work (is there a fee for that)? How do I leave that system? You can start a discussion on the Self Storage Income Facebook or Instagram groups to learn from other people's experiences.

Also, how does the PMS tie into your gate system, your security system? You need to know these things before you upgrade your facility so it all works together. For example, do you use a gate system from one company and then use a separate self storage manager software for your PMS—and do those two things talk? If not, it's going to be a problem. How do tenants get access? How do you lock people out when they don't pay? You want to automate those things. If they don't pay . . . CLICK . . . they're locked out. It's important.

FACILITY UPGRADES

Design your facility upgrade to supply what is most in demand and to look nicer than the highest quality competition. Have your branding strategy in place during the planning stage of the upgrades, so you present a consistent look throughout. Upgrade the showroom, lighting, security, and automation systems that will interface with your PMS (property management system) software.

Complete the upgrade work as soon as possible, and hire and train your staff while it's in progress. Also, as soon as you have signed the papers on the purchase, and before you've completed the facility upgrades, raise rates to turn out price-conscious tenants. Draft your policies and procedures, consult with your legal team on the lease agreement language, and get marketing on board.

Curb Appeal and Showroom

Curb appeal has to do with the front entrance look, fencing, and landscaping. This may be a large or small capital expenditure, depending on both its current state and how you want it to look when finished. You will need to work with the city planning department to obtain approval on the design of all street-facing structures.

The showroom is usually part of a larger capital expenditure, but the same things apply—if it was big enough but unappealing it may be more of a cosmetic facelift. Every situation is different.

As an example, below is a "before" photo of Storage Investment #3 as purchased with our signs on it.

Storage Investment #3 "before" appearance.

Here is the same facility's office after renovations:

Storage Investment #3 after renovations.

Security

Security is a critical part of creating a self storage facility that quality-conscious tenants want to use. It must be tied into the front entrance gate, fencing, the showroom and office, and all units.

Gate Access

Gate access ideally should be tied into the PMS and require codes for each tenant.

Camera Monitoring

First, make sure the cameras are real. It's surprising how often people put up fake cameras. Make sure the cameras record the footage with high enough resolution to see license plates and faces. Look out for hidden dark spots that cameras can't see into. Make sure your lighting allows adequate illumination for the cameras and put them where they will see people coming and going—cover all entrances and exits.

Alarm Center

For after-hours security alarms, any alarms go to an after-hours call center that is part of your security service.

OPTIMIZE OPERATIONS

The PMS software you buy to help you run the facility will be a key component in optimizing operations and training employees. To find out what other self storage managers are doing, join the Self Storage Income Facebook and Instagram groups.

Important steps to cover in setting up your operations include these:

1. Coordinate selecting a PMS with the technology and security upgrades you intend to implement.
2. Draft your policies and procedures with revenue management in mind (see Revenue Management section).

3. Select third-party vendors and key team members. Here are some of the important ones:
    a. Accounting
    b. Marketing
    c. Legal
    d. Technical support for website and software systems
    e. Collections
4. Set up employee training resources and processes.
5. Look for opportunities to lower expenses:
    a. Set up annual maintenance plans on equipment to limit larger repairs.
    b. Reach out to contractors and have them bid against one another to be your preferred contractor for your facility.
    c. Set up systems for tracking and reducing delinquencies.
    d. Consider hiring a service to handle evictions and auctions. These can save a lot of time, minimize the time a unit isn't producing rent, and reduce legal risk.
6. Join a self storage association to learn more about best practices and trends in operations improvements. There may be both state and national organizations to choose from.

See more details on these aspects in the following sections.

MANAGING YOUR CUSTOMERS

The management of customers inside your facility either makes or breaks a facility. Customer service is of primary importance. Remember that women are the primary decision makers; you need to set things up to make them feel safe, secure, and comfortable.

Remodel the office so it smells good, looks good, feels safe, and has visible security cameras. Customers need to know they are safe and their stuff is safe.

Customer Service

How does the manager treat the customer? The manager should be smiling, offer popcorn and bottled water, and make the customer feel the manager is engaged in the process. Especially in overbuilt markets, it's essential to have excellent customer service.

Think about the whole consumer experience from the customer's point of view: finding the facility online, going inside the showroom, making the decision to purchase. Work to connect all those things together. The middle stage, visiting the facility, is where the decision is made.

If the manager is off-putting, that's a big no-no. We hire a manager who knows how to treat people. Our managers offer to take customers out in a clean golf cart to show them the facility.

Other things, such as rodent control, are important for customers to see. Offering a more customized service is a great way to compete against REITs.

Value is largely perception. If the customer doesn't perceive value, it doesn't matter what you say—they aren't going to buy.

The Sales Process

Our policy requires insurance for all tenants and because we offer tenant insurance, most will buy from us.

We also offer products such as wraps, pallets, and boxes—these things are cheaper at Walmart, a few miles away, but customers don't want to go there and come back. With a remodeled office and upgraded facilities, people are willing to pay.

Other than the add-ons mentioned above, there's only two ways to increase revenue: increase price per SF and increase the length of stay.

Remember the three different types of customers. We go after the quality customer who will pay more. They will not buy unless you are offering these extras. The experience is part of that. It helps to differentiate us from the competition.

Offering those upgrades will also get rid of the price-conscious customer.

Call Center for 24/7 Access

Service is not limited to daily hours. You need to have service available 24 hours a day. The manager isn't on-site 24/7, so contract with a call center to take care of billing details and access the site, especially for new customers. The call center is also available to cover for the manager if someone calls while they are out with another customer.

EMPLOYEE TRAINING

This is an opportunity to set up the employee and facility for success. We show employees how the home office fits into the process as much as possible (our home office is in Boise, and unless they are in the area, they don't see it). We also give them as many resources as possible, including an online training center with videos and PDFs.

We also tell them what decisions they should be making when the tenants ask for certain things, like if the tenant wants to live in their unit, they know to say they can't do that. We have people set up as assistant trainers for questions. We have mock practice for certain scenarios so they understand how they should respond.

As a trainer, you don't want to make the mistake of assuming that, because you communicated the info to the employee, they know it. The scenarios allow them to practice so they do understand it even before the tenant comes in.

Setting up a communication and organization tool such as Basecamp (free) or something similar can help to keep communications open and organized.

LEGAL

Take serious steps to avoid lawsuits. This starts at move-in—get all signatures on all forms before the tenant moves in.

Train employees to take detailed notes in the electronic file in four areas for all customer interactions:

1. Who attempted to contact
2. Why contact was made
3. What was said
4. What follow-up was needed

We also make sure to have authorized contacts for a unit—the tenant themselves and an authorized third party if they designate one. So we have a verification process employees can use in person and over the phone to make sure we are talking to an authorized person.

We also provide specific language employees should use in the event that a tenant starts a lawsuit. As soon as a tenant says they are going to consult legal action, employees can only tell them what the balance on their account is and then refer them to the legal team. That allows us to control the communication—so that what and how it is said is controlled by legal. We also take security very seriously; we have cameras in place and lock up every night, making sure we are keeping information that's useful to anyone (identity, etc.) locked up and not available to anyone who wants to take advantage.

Lien Process

Whenever we take over a facility, we find a lot of tenants who are in the facility who shouldn't be because they haven't paid. We have found that the lien process intimidates many facility managers, so they don't use it and just let the tenant stay.

To make the lien process one you can use, you have to follow some steps:

1. On signing paperwork, you get the tenant's signature that they agree a lien process could eventually happen.
2. Have them declare if they are active duty military. This is important because active duty servicemembers are eligible for the SMCRA (service members civil relief act), which requires a different process before auctioning their unit.
3. You need to know if they are storing a vehicle because often there are separate procedures for vehicles—you need to know if there's a lien on that vehicle or if you have title and registration. Whenever a vehicle, trailer, boat, or camper is stored that requires registration, we have to have a copy of proof of ownership such as the title and also a copy of current registration. There are often separate lien procedures for the sale of vehicles.
4. If they are storing a vehicle, make sure the vehicle is always in the tenant's name. **Do not accept storage of a vehicle by anyone other than the title holder.** If there is a preexisting lien on the vehicle, you do not have legal recourse with that vehicle if you can't speak to the owner of the vehicle. Our contracts require all lienholders of any property stored in our facilities to be disclosed. This is not limited to only ve-

hicles but can be things like rent-to-own furniture or work equipment. Lienholders have to be contacted before sale can be conducted.

5. From the very beginning, when payment is late we call the tenant consistently to inform them that rent is due, so we don't get into lien status. When we call consistently, fewer people end up in that situation.

6. When a unit is going to be auctioned, we make sure to have two employees participate in any unit inventory so they can verify the process was followed, serve as witnesses to each other, and make sure that no processes were broken.

7. Occasionally a tenant will file for bankruptcy. When this happens, the paperwork will be mailed to the facility. It should immediately be put in the priority notes in the property management system to alert everyone working that it is a bankruptcy and the paperwork should be placed in the tenant's file. Bankruptcies can vary by judgement and can be difficult to understand. All contact with the tenant, collections attempts, and lien processing should cease until you can clarify with your attorney.

The Best Solution for Liens: Hire Someone

The biggest change we made to our operations that streamlined the lien process was hiring a third-party company to handle liens and auctions. Their job is to make sure all the default notices that are required by state law in each of the four states where we do business are done on time and as required to be fully legal. Each state has a different set of timelines. The language used in our vendor's notices doesn't pull any punches and is very direct with what date the tenant's belongings will be auctioned if they don't pay in time. Their service also puts all documents needed on file. The entire lien process takes one to five weeks.

TENANT DOCUMENTATION AT MOVE-IN

There's no more important time to get the documentation in place than when the tenant moves in. We make sure the documentation is in order. We tell employees to treat each tenant as if this is the one that will sue them. Here's the system we use:

1. We have a checklist for the process to make sure everything is covered.

2. We make sure we are setting up that tenant for autopay. We promote this through *assuming the sale*—we don't tell them we accept cash and checks. We tell them we do autopay billing and ask what credit card they would like to use. We get them all signed up on the first day. Then we have very little reason to contact them unless the card doesn't go through. We also have a setup for online payment that isn't automated.

3. We make sure the tenants sign up for tenant insurance. When something goes wrong, the tenant wants someone to pay and they don't care who it is. We assume the sale for this too by telling them what the rent is with the insurance, assuming the basic insurance policy is included. We also require that our tenants carry insurance—it doesn't have to be our insurance, but we require proof and they don't usually have that, so they sign up. We tell them we will take ours off if and when they bring in proof of theirs.

Another option we use for our fully automated facilities is an online move-in system which includes online signing of all required documents. There are several services like this and it ensures everything is signed with no mistakes.

TENANT MOVE-OUTS

If there's one place we lose money, it's the move-out process. Tenants are not likely to pay us anymore if they have all their stuff. Collections are a losing proposition, as we only get a fraction of the money we lost—so revenue management in this case is doing what we can to prevent the collection process in the first place.

We tell tenants there are four things that have to happen before we remove the tenant from their financial and legal responsibility:

1. Unit needs to be empty.
2. Lock needs to be removed.
3. Paperwork must be signed.
4. Their balance needs to be paid.

If a unit has been abandoned and we feel the tenant does not want to come back and remove their items, we send a notice of abandonment so the responsibility for the items and unit is removed but the financial responsibility is not. This gets a pretty good response as people don't want that balance to grow.

PRORATING POLICY CHANGE

A few years ago, we changed our prorating policy: if people moved out in the first few days of the month, instead of giving them a refund on the remainder of the month (which basically forces us to send any potential tenant to our competitors *and* lose that month's rent when we refund the existing tenant), we make it a requirement that they must give us five days' notice. If we know that they intend to move out, we could plan on that unit being empty.

That way, we could tell new tenants one was coming open and put them on the waiting list instead of sending them away. Also, we don't state in our contract that we do refunds or prorates at all, and that protects us—if they fail to give the five days' notice, they can't argue with paying for the whole month because they signed an agreement that does not promise refunds. We also make sure we research the refund policy on a case-by-case basis, so we aren't refunding every single tenant who asks.

REVENUE MANAGEMENT

Look at self storage like a business and focus on revenue management. How much does it cost to get a tenant? What's that tenant willing to pay? How much will they pay? How long will they stay? If you have those basic things, you can figure out the overall *lifetime value* of a tenant.

THE LIFETIME VALUE OF A CUSTOMER

The concept of the lifetime value of a customer (tenant) is an important one that will guide a lot of strategic thinking as you learn the self storage industry. The spread between cost of acquisition (how much you spend to get the customer in the door) and the lifetime value of the customer (the average monthly rent for the facility times the average length of stay), will tell you how much each customer is really worth. Then the questions to ask are: Can I lower the cost of acquisition? Can I increase the customer's lifetime value? Can I lower our fixed and variable costs to increase profit per customer? These are the metrics on which I've learned to focus.

We learned very quickly that some tenants have a lifetime value in a 10 x 10 unit of $1,500 when others had a lifetime value of $3,000. We want to get the ones with the $3,000 lifetime value because the cost to obtain a tenant changes based on the marketing pay per click, but the building cost is fixed. It's not variable. So your profit goes up when you target the tenants with the $3,000 lifetime value.

CRAFT POLICIES AND PROCEDURES TO MAXIMIZE REVENUE

Your policies directly impact how much you make off of each tenant. Put rules in place with that in mind:

- Set up a system for managing delinquencies that is consistently enforced.
- Present autopay as the default payment method during tenant onboarding, not an option. This will reduce delinquencies and has been shown statistically to increase length of stay.
- Require tenant insurance. They will buy from you because of the convenience. Self-funding the insurance policies is an option that can maximize profit.
- Require five days' notice when they want to move out, or they must pay the entire month's rent.
- Do not state in the lease contract that you will refund a month's rent if they move out early.
- Offer add-on products for convenience to the customer: boxes, pallets, bed sheets. They will buy from you to save time rather than run down the road.
- Plan for regular rate increases and have a system for doing that.

MANAGING DELINQUENCIES

This is one case where the policies you set will impact your bottom line. Set policies with reminders and deadlines and hold to them.

1. Establish policies for due dates and late fees and consistently enforce them. Take that responsibility away from local facility managers.
2. Promote autopay as the standard setup.
3. Be courteous but firm.
4. Have a policy for eviction and auctions and enforce them.

Auctions

When a unit's contents need to be auctioned, have a standard procedure such as this:

1. Inventory the unit (you need to know there is something to sell and it's not empty). This is important if you have bidders showing up in person.
2. Consider an online auction process. We transitioned to this and it was a smart move—time spent on auctions went down and profit went up. It took a lot of time, if 30 bidders showed up, to sign them all in and then conduct the auction, while you could lose a new tenant who happened to walk in as that was happening because you couldn't serve them.
   We take detailed photos and post them online, which better promotes the unit. Online bidding is more efficient: bidders can bid over one to two weeks at their convenience; the auction functions like eBay although bidders buy the whole unit. There are fewer bidders because they can see better if they really want it or not. An online form takes care of the winning bidder and the details of signing up.

RATE MANAGEMENT: DON'T FORGET INFLATION

You lose 3% every year to inflation. So a 6% return is really a 3% return. This is called adjusted risk in financial planning. When you look at your overall return, you have to factor in this erosion of your income for any long-term planning.

The government is incentivized to create inflation. They have to—if there's no inflation, we're all in big trouble. Deflation means depression. So every year, your standard of living needs to rise, and your investment incomes need to rise. You need to be able to raise the rental rates in your storage facility every year.

If your rental rates are not appreciating every year to compensate, in 20 years it doesn't do the trick. You see that in certain markets in the United States. It's called deflation. Detroit's a perfect example—many houses sell for less today than they did 30 years ago. And this is happening all over the Midwest—anywhere that there's stagnation in the economy. The month-to-month nature of self storage makes it easy to raise rates, however you need to know what the market will bear and have a safety margin built into your plan.

MANAGING THE LIFETIME VALUE OF A TENANT

The concept of a lifetime value sets the basis for a lot of strategic thinking and planning.

$$\text{Rate} \times \text{length of stay (LOS)} - \text{unit cost} = \text{profit}$$

This calculation can show you the ROI on your marketing budget and other information, depending on how you calculate it. Understanding what makes tenants stay should be part of your facility upgrade decisions and revenue management policies.

Your marketing can target those customers who are the best long-term value—the ones who will stay the longest. This is a critical part of the calculation to understand what a tenant is worth to you.

How can you increase the lifetime value of each customer?

1. Decrease costs (this is hard; these are usually fixed)
2. Increase the rate
3. Increase the length of time they stay

If you increase quality, convenience, and security, you can increase your price. Then you can increase the length of stay if the tenants are happy with what you provide. So everything about the way you set up your business should help tenants stay longer.

You need to find the value in your operations and then maximize it. In terms of keeping tenants, your facility needs to be attractive to the quality-conscious tenants as they will stay longer; they are not transitional. They are the homeowner who wants the storage unit to be an extension of their home. So appearance, security, and updating are first. Marketing to target those people is a huge part of this; more on that in the next section. The units themselves are next. Price them based on square footage, not per item. So a 10 x 10 costs four times as much as a 5 x 5.

The add-on products described next are also ways to increase a customer's lifetime value.

ADD-ON PRODUCTS

The biggest add-on is insurance. Different types of storage are also add-ons— extra amenities like climate control specifically for wine storage, document storage, and gun storage. Or enclosed storage with power for collectible automobiles or other vehicles that need a trickle charger.

Additional products include boxes, bed sheets, and the pallets to keep items off the ground. Pallets in particular are a real moneymaker for us because they are essentially free and we rent them out to tenants for $2 per month or sell them directly. Everybody buys them and then leaves them there—so we can collect them and sell them again.

MARKETING

Marketing is a great advantage in self storage because most of the competition in third-tier markets or facilities owned by individuals may not be keeping up with the times and aren't taking advantage of it. They may have a Yellow Pages listing or a static landing page with no functionality—but no Google visibility at all. For my facilities, 90% of our customer traffic comes from online searches. We do get some drive-by traffic, but often they will look you up online as a result of that, and it's still the online presence that brings them in.

Marketing is a fantastic value-add for a self storage facility. Step one is to think about the three types of customers:

1. Price conscious: These tenants are often messy and don't pay their bills. So collections go up.

2. Location-centric: These tenants are the low-hanging fruit most self storage facilities focus on.

3. Quality conscious: These tenants are willing to pay the highest price.

When you are not marketing, you're only getting two of the three types of customers—the first and the second. You're missing the ones who are willing to pay the most. The difference can be a 30% increase in fees and a massive revenue increase. You need to upgrade your facility with these tenants in mind and focus your marketing on them.

How you market also depends on where your occupancy rates are. Once you reach a certain occupancy, your online marketing expenditures should be reduced. You don't need to work that hard at that point. And if your occupancy is dropping, you need to increase your pay per clicks. This is part of customizing your marketing strategies to maximize revenue.

HIRE A THIRD-PARTY VENDOR FOR MARKETING

This is one area where I strongly suggest you hire a third-party company that specializes in self storage and can manage your pay-per-click strategies effectively.

STRENGTHEN BRANDING

Part of your visibility is having a brand identity. Create a brand around your facility and incorporate it into your upgrades and operations.

- Get a logo
- Update signage
- Institute an employee dress code and/or uniform
- Update employee training with a focus on customer service
- Update your facility's office, showroom, and curb appeal
- Update value proposition and product offerings

UPGRADE YOUR ONLINE PRESENCE

Operating a self storage facility is really about managing two locations: the facility itself and its online presence.

- Build a website (it *must* be mobile-friendly)

- Optimize your website to allow users to do these things easily:
  - Locate your facility
  - Make payments
  - Contact you

Improve your website's SEO (search engine optimization) with digital content such as helpful and informative blog posts, articles, and videos.

RAISE RATES TO MATCH VALUE

Your tenants' monthly rental rates should reflect and match the value you are now providing with your facility. Your due diligence data will provide you with guidelines for what the rate should be.

You can do this immediately on taking ownership, even before you have upgraded the facility. See the second part of the Storage Investment #4 case study at the end of this chapter for how we did this.

ATTRACTING YOUR DREAM TENANT

Who are you trying to attract? In an industry that operates on month-to-month leases, the longer a tenant stays, the more they are worth.

I know that 65% of the people who make the decision to choose self storage are female. I also know the longest-staying tenants own a house. So my dream client is a female homeowner. The man may do the moving, but she makes the decision. The nicer and more secure the facility, the more stable and longer-staying tenants you will have. If she's not comfortable, she won't stay. Quality is number one—think of the storage unit as an extension of their house.

Obviously revenue management and marketing are interrelated, and the lifetime value of a tenant was covered in the revenue management section— but the ideas need to be revisited when you create your marketing strategies. You need to know how much a tenant is worth so you can decide how much to spend in marketing to get them. The calculation for the lifetime value of a tenant gives you that number.

How to Increase the Lifetime Value of a Tenant

Do an audit of your facility. Look at the units, and look at the tenants who a) simply paid an 8% price increase; b) didn't complain; and c) didn't leave. Those are your dream tenants. Why? They are not very elastic; they are there to stay and price isn't the primary driver for them. They like your facility and what you provide.

Apartment dwellers stay for a shorter period of time and they are more price conscious. They are not my dream tenant, so my marketing does not target them. You want to target your dream tenants and choose the highest-paying tenants because there's limited capacity.

I know that my average dream tenant is worth thousands of dollars because they are willing to pay higher prices and their length of stay is longer. For most of the facilities we buy, the lifetime value customer at the time of purchase is under $2,000—and that's not my dream tenant. I plan everything to get my dream tenant in there. My value calculation in deciding to buy a facility is based on that dream tenant.

Dynamic Pricing Based on Type of Client

Storage facility operators sell much more than units. Using the right software, they can use dynamic pricing, just like the hotel industry. If you've ever been on an airplane and asked three people next to you what they paid for their hotel room, you'll get answers like this: one paid a $100, one paid $5, and another paid $500. That's how self storage is operated too, because demand is constantly changing.

Data Aggregation

This is a paid service that provides data on customers, market demands, and trends. It is useful for evaluating a market. It can also be used to target the customers you want and hide from the ones you don't want. We use these services regularly.

Here are more details about how we successfully transitioned the Storage Investment #4 facility I mentioned in the previous chapter to maximize its revenue and value.

CASE STUDY: STORAGE INVESTMENT #4 PART II

The Storage Investment #4 facility we purchased a few years ago from the state of Idaho was a 75K SF, underperforming asset. Our initial evaluation of that facility is described in the previous chapter. The day we bought the facility, we sent out an email to all of the customers saying their rent was going up—somewhere between a 65% to more than 100% increase. A huge percentage of the current tenants left—over 35%. This was in February. We evicted all nonpaying tenants and put $150,000 into facility upgrades and another $50,000 into resealing. By early summer, we had replaced all of those low-paying tenants with higher paying tenants.

Our revenue skyrocketed. Our valuation increased by millions in a matter of months just with advertising and this value-add strategy of going after the quality customer.

Two years later, that asset is worth around $9M and is about a 7.5 cap. We are sitting at below 50% debt to equity (D/E). If we wanted, we could refinance to remove our money. The returns would be infinite from that point on because we would have our investment capital back.

The Storage Investment #4 facility was a rate and market discrepancy opportunity we knew how to take advantage of. We knew we could increase the revenue through our value-add strategy and processes.

KEY TAKEAWAYS

▶ Find what brings value to your business. Plan capital improvements around that value and to attract your ideal tenant.

▶ Focus on getting the add-on products, revenue increase strategies, and delinquencies under control with clear policies to actively manage your revenue.

CHAPTER 8

How to Reduce Risk

There is always risk. How can you bring it down as low as possible?

First, understand that not all risk is created equal. In general in the business world, the greater the potential returns, the greater the risk.

Reducing risk is about minimizing your exposure to the investment.

You want to place an organization between you and the risk—a simple example is dividend stocks.

A dividend stock might pay you a set fee of 3% for owning the shares. The worst that can happen is you lose your 3% and the initial investment. You don't go under if Apple goes under, for example. You benefit from the dividends and reinvestment, plus the market value of your shares increases. You can increase your return by the compounding effect of reinvesting your dividends.

If you want a return of 5-8%, that is low risk and only your capital is at risk. An example is a diversified portfolio in the open markets.

Let's look at storage facilities. As a real estate asset class, storage has higher risk than you might think. They are an intermediate-risk investment. Storage facilities operate on month-to-month leases. It's much more variable and operates on shorter time frames than an apartment building and other real estate assets. That can be a benefit but it's also a risk. A tenant can decide to move out tomorrow. Self storage has a much higher turnover rate than an apartment building, retail, or housing.

For commercial retail and office buildings, the risk is high. If a commercial building has two tenants and one of them leaves, your revenue drops by half—contract or no. It's a big risk. You see these buildings empty all the time.

KNOWLEDGE AND EXPERIENCE CAN REDUCE RISK

A valuable point in this discussion is that part of the risk to me in investing in retail and office real estate is that I have no skill in the office and retail industry—I don't know what I'm doing. Knowledge can reduce my risk.

For an apartment building, I would put in a third-party manager and get a 10-12% return. So I don't have to know what I'm doing.

In self storage, if you know what you're doing, you can be an active investor and manage the capital and revenue flows. I do this and I get much higher returns: 15-25%. My standard is 20% or more. I don't take anything projected at less than that. For me, it's lower risk because I know what I'm doing.

KNOW YOUR MARKET AND HOW TO IDENTIFY A VALUE-ADD OPPORTUNITY

No matter how you intend to enter the market, your success is in jeopardy if you don't do your due diligence. This includes researching the local market in terms of current rates and your competitor's offerings and occupancy rates.

A critical thing to know is that you must avoid overbuilt markets, especially for your first investment in self storage. The competition can be brutal, and you may not come out ahead. So the first answers you need about any new market are how saturated is the local market and what kind of tenants does it serve. If they are all price-conscious tenants in run-down facilities, there may be an opportunity to offer something for quality-conscious tenants, especially if the five-mile radius includes subdivisions with the homeowner customers who will pay the higher price.

> # If you can recognize an underperforming asset, that reduces your risk.

If you know the local market, the state of supply and demand, and what kind of rates the competition is charging, you know what is possible. With a few key pieces of information (such as occupancy rates of the competition, data about the number of homeowners in the local market, and what kind of units are in greater demand), there may be very little risk in leveraging your capital with a high debt/equity ratio because you *know* you will be able to increase the profitability of the facility dramatically, in a short period of time.

SEPARATION FROM THE RISK THROUGH BUSINESS ORGANIZATION

One form of protection is to separate the asset ownership by creating an LLC. This protects you from lawsuits, but you still have a personal guarantee with your borrowed money—whether it's a bank, credit union, or your family—so you are still on the hook for that money.

My method is to put two layers of organization between me and the risk. This is done by establishing a separate LLC to own each location in your portfolio. If you intend to own more than one, set up a parent LLC as a holding entity and assign revenues from each of the individual asset LLCs to this parent. This is a two-tiered LLC.

I place ownership of every one of my storage facilities in an LLC—a separate LLC for each asset. Then I have a holdings company and every time the LLC produces a profit, the profit is pulled out of the LLC and put into a second LLC, the holdings company (mine is Bitterroot Holdings). So each self storage business is isolated and can only be sued for what they have. And that doesn't touch the assets of the holdings company.

For real estate investors, here's the best way to protect yourself: Buy an asset and put it in an LLC. Improve the asset's profitability and refinance it to get the initial capital expenditure back. Then, refinance into a *non-recourse loan*. This is usually a CMBS (commercial mortgage-backed securities) loan. The capital is then protected, and the holdings company is protected from lawsuits. The CMBS loan protects you from the bank.

A CMBS loan product takes your loan and puts it into a big package of real estate assets' debt. Say it's $50 million worth. That $50 million goes on the bond market as a bond—the debt market. This debt is collateralized into a CMBS loan. This means they cannot go after me if I default. The asset is the collateral and if I default, I give the bank the asset. Essentially, I defer that risk onto the bond holders.

C/I/B

Another way to look at risk is to look at the three elements of risk: loss of your capital (C), risk of being sued by individuals (I), and the bank (B).

To protect your capital, refinance the now-profitable asset and get your money back—although there are caveats to that, which I'll discuss in the next chapter, on knowing when to sell or scale. That's (C). To protect yourself from being sued by individuals (I), set up a two-tiered LLC as I described above—an LLC for each asset that delivers the profits to a second holding company LLC. To protect yourself from the bank (B), use a non-recourse CMBS loan to do the refinance.

RISK IN LEVERAGING YOUR CAPITAL

Leveraging capital is how you build a real estate portfolio. It involves investing a small amount of cash and taking on a large amount of debt. The more you leverage your cash, the more property you can buy. The higher the debt to equity ratio, the higher your payments will be and the greater the risk that the revenue won't cover the payments.

KEY TAKEAWAYS

▶ Understand that not all risk is equal.

▶ At a minimum, establish a separate LLC for each facility you own. If you own more than one, establish a holding company and direct revenue from each individual LLC to the holding company. Litigation cannot reach the holding company, only the assets in the individual LLCs.

▶ Risk is reduced in any investment when you understand the markets and what creates value.

CHAPTER 9

Static Real Estate Asset to Dynamic Self Storage Business

WHAT'S NEXT? YOUR ACTIONABLE STEPS

Okay, so you've successfully executed on these steps:

- Saved money and/or raised money
- Identified a market and a facility
- Performed market research and due diligence
- Purchased a storage facility
- Increased the value of your facility

So what now?

If you know me at all by now, you know I would suggest to you to rinse and repeat.

This leads to the next topic: what's the best way to get capital from your first facility so you can buy another?

KNOWING WHEN TO SELL OR SCALE

First, what is your essential goal? There is no wrong answer. It depends on what you want to achieve. Your basic options are these:

1. Refinance:

- If you went the owner finance route when you purchased the facility, refinancing at your facility's new value after your improvements can be a great way to deploy that equity to pay off the owner completely.
- You can refinance no matter how you financed the initial purchase, if your D/E ratio is good enough and you can still maintain a margin of safety.

2. Get line of credit on the facility:

- Obtaining a line of credit on your facility can allow you to use that capital:
  - To perform additional renovations
  - To purchase another storage facility

3. Accumulate cash:

- If refinancing or getting a line of credit on your facility doesn't make sense, you can simply accumulate revenue and save up cash for any of these purposes:
  - Purchase another facility
  - Buy out the owner (if you owner financed)
  - Perform additional renovations

4. Sell:

- Selling is an option when your goal is a different kind (or size) of facility than the one you have now. Sometimes in life things change and that's okay. Just be aware of taxes that result from the sale.

What follows are more specifics on these four options.

1. REFINANCING

This is a powerful tool when you are operating a value-add strategy. You can get a lower cap rate, get better loan terms, get your money out, and do it again. If you seller-financed the original purchase, it's a great way to pay off the original owner and take the cash for your next investment. All the same information about relationships and trust in working with financiers obviously all apply to refinancing.

Example Return on Investment with Refinancing

Consider the opportunity presented by the facility shown in the chart below, for example. When we found it, it was 100% occupied and 95K SF, but its rates were substantially below market. This purchase was a home run.

For this example, let's say you invested $100K with us on this deal. The facility was worth $6M at a 7 cap. We put 30% down ($1.8M).

	Year 1	Year 2	Year 3	Year 4	Year 5
Return on $100K investment	$12,768	$14,850	$158,866	$11,089	$13,685
Cumulative return	$12,768	$27,618	$186,484	$197,573	$211,259
Cash on cash return	12.77%	14.85%	158.87%	11.09%	13.69%
Cumulative cash on cash	12.77%	27.62%	186.48%	197.57%	211.26%
IRR	-87.23%	-54.55%	24.49%	27.5%	29.3%

Let's look at what happened with the facility after purchase and the power of refinancing for your rate of return. The first two or three years, we increased rates up to market, which you can see as your return as your $100K grows.

By year 3, the revenue had grown substantially and so did the value. This is where the opportunity lies. You can go to the bank and refinance at the same 70/30 ratio you did at the beginning. You can also use a non-recourse loan. This does three things:

1. Your debt increases because of the new larger loan.
2. But your ability to pay it increases too because the revenues increased at the same proportion. So your risk of not making debt payments has not changed.
3. You lowered your risk because you were able to get your money back that you invested. Now your returns are infinite because you already received 100% return. You're now playing with the house's money!

You can also lower your risk through a non-recourse loan, meaning if the asset fails, you're not liable—the bank is. Unless you do something illegal.

The chart shows the refinance to get your money out occurring in year 3 by adding your $100K back to your return on investment in the first line, and also the over 100% returns on the second and third lines in the chart.

Did your mind just explode? Your risk has been reduced to almost nothing and you still own it and are getting cashflow and tax benefits. The first time someone walked me though this, my mind *did* explode. I couldn't believe there's a whole world of people doing this and few people know. This is why I love real estate.

When you decide to refinance, a great way to reduce risk is to obtain a CMBS loan or work with insurance companies, but these can have more hoops and fees. The less you want to risk (the greater the percentage of the purchase price you intend to finance), the worse those terms are going to be. A few banks do specialize in self storage and will help you out. Also there are attorneys who specialize in self storage.

Refinancing Is Not Always the Best Option

Just because you can refinance doesn't mean you should, in every case. Evaluate the facility to make sure revenues and the valuation have stabilized and that you still have a margin of safety in case the market drops. However, refinancing can be a great catalyst for growth and a way to reduce risk.

A lot of people say, "I did this and I got my money back and I took the risk off the table." But if you are still the guarantor on the loan, you didn't really take the risk off the table. You just shifted it—so make sure you understand that. If you take the money out and get a loan on another property, that is diversifying the risk but it's not taking it away. And by leveraging a property, you trade larger monthly profits and a more conservative investment portfolio for a larger portfolio and a potentially more diverse and maybe riskier one.

You need to stress test your portfolio. Understand how the asset will perform under different market conditions. What if your occupancy drops from 90% to 80%? In that scenario, it's not a simple case of lower occupancy. In that case, you will be giving more rental discounts to bring in more tenants—so your revenue will drop more than that simple drop in occupancy would predict. In a bad economy, you will also have more people who are not paying—so your picture will change in terms of several aspects. To get people back in, you've got to cut rates. You need to play with scenarios using likely situations.

When you choose to refinance is important too. As I mentioned, make sure the revenue and valuation have stabilized before taking this step. You have to be comfortable that the facility is going to survive.

When and if you do it also depends on your goals. For us, we want good stable assets with low risk. The way for us to reduce risk is to increase our margin. So we have very strict rules.

Our rules include these things: a 20% IRR (internal rate of return), at a minimum. And all of our facilities are much higher than that. That's our MOS—margin of safety.

The less experienced you are, the more important this is.

This is why REITs buy in certain types of markets. They want to reduce their risk on certain markets—say a first-tier market where it's nearly impossible to build another storage facility nearby—and they will pay a really low cap rate to get this. If you are in a second-, third-, or fourth-tier market, 90% of the markets do not have that. Say you have a 5 cap facility in a third-tier market and someone builds down the road from you, where there's a population of 15K people. You are in trouble. You have to have a margin of safety.

There are some great reasons to refinance. If you needed to get a deal done so you sacrificed on the terms of your loan, refinancing to be in a better financial and legal situation is a great reason to refinance. We do that and we suggest it because markets change in cycles; if you're at the top of a market and credit is easy, terms are loose; if you're at the bottom of a market, credit is really tight and terms are not good. They can be bad. Refinancing can improve your loan terms.

2. OBTAIN A LINE OF CREDIT ON YOUR FIRST FACILITY

There's a much easier way to get your money instead of selling: borrow on your equity and use that for reinvestment. You don't have to pay taxes on that money like you would if you sold. And you still have the first asset and the revenue it is producing.

3. ACCUMULATE CASH FROM REVENUE

In lower-tier markets, we prefer to grow on cash flow rather than return on equity (refinancing to get your money out). Be cash-flow rich, and then you can use other strategies to purchase additional facilities. We use lines of credit that are accessible and then pay off that with cash flow rather than refinancing, for many scenarios.

One thing to add: it always comes down to your strategy and why you are purchasing it in the first place. We accumulate cash from revenue because we are operating the business and want to increase performance. However, we do refinance, once the revenues have stabilized, and have refinanced more than 80% of our facilities.

4. SELL

First of all, if you have a value-add strategy or you want passive income, you get those funds up front when you sell. We have sold some of our assets—and where markets get out of whack and you want to reduce your risk, it's a good option.

If you want to grow your capital rapidly, you can capitalize on the increased value you've created by selling and investing the returns in a larger facility using a 1031 exchange. We have used this growth strategy successfully. You are trading up to the type of facility that produces the revenue you want.

There's also the sell price versus the buy price. Let's say you have a 5 cap and, all other things being equal, you know you can buy the exact same value as an 8 cap. I would take that deal. And we've done that. If you sell, you have to do something with that money. Either you reallocate it (using a 1031 exchange) or you pay taxes. This is not a good option when the market is super high. You can't reallocate easily or for the same value . . . if you are willing to sell high and then wait, that could work. However, that doesn't work for me and this is why: at the end of the day, markets always go up in the long term. In the short term, there are fluctuations. But those fluctuations could last decades. You can't time the market. I would highly suggest you not try to do that.

When I sold, I did so for good reasons and it worked out. The reason was to get out of an asset I didn't want. If you started really small and want a bigger facility, sell the small one and move up. It could look like this:

Put $100K into a $500K asset; sell it and take $250K out and buy into a $1M asset, then take $450-$500K out and put it into a $3M asset, sell it and take $1.5M out and put into a $4M asset. Once you are up to that level and you only buy $5M-plus assets, you don't get the wide spread—the velocity of money—in going from a $500K asset to a $4 million asset. Your growth is different.

As another example, I bought a $7M asset that's now worth over $20 million, and if it gets too crazy I will sell that because I look at it like this: If the money difference in the spread ($7M to $25M = $18M) is more than 10 years' worth of income, I have to seriously take that into consideration. All of a sudden, when it becomes 15 or 20 years' worth of income, I have to look at that. But I also look at the payback time—how much time would that asset take to pay back that price and replacement cost?

So if that asset makes $250K per year but I can sell it and buy five facilities that will make $400K per year, that makes sense. But once again, I look to see if I can take out a loan against that. If I borrow against that and I make $100K *and* I can buy three facilities that will make me $300K, I am still at $400K per year with less risk. I didn't have all that cash out there that I had to use to either buy something quick or pay taxes on; when I do that, I'm taking the risk that I can find the assets that will meet my criteria so I can achieve that. Or it takes me five years to find them and they're worth more, and my cash flow is lower than when I began *and* I paid taxes. That's the risk.

And remember the economy changes, sometimes very unexpectedly.

So you sell to trade up. I'm fine with that but you'll get to a point where you can use equity to do more. There's a difference between size and quantity. If you want to move up in size of asset or markets, selling makes sense.

If you are looking to move up in quantity, go with equity. You'll increase your cash flow faster that way.

Again, markets change. In five years, this argument could look different. But these are the thought processes you should use to decide whether to sell or scale. Risk is the unknown and you need to make sure you are not assuming that you'll be able to repeat what you just did. Consider the risk and what could happen if you can't do what you plan.

HOW TO BUILD AN EMPIRE

This was my ultimate goal, but it may or may not be yours. Even if you just want to own two facilities, all of this information applies.

Now that you have learned how to grow value in your first facility, go find another facility and do the same process as many times as you want.

If you want to buy another facility in a small market, be sure that the additional small facilities you buy are in *other* small markets or cities. Do not invest in the same small market or city more than once. This helps to diversify your storage portfolio across similar, but different markets. This is especially important in small markets as they can be extremely volatile and are generally hypersensitive to market downturns.

After growing your portfolio to three to four facilities, use the cashflow and/or equity from those facilities through line of credit or refinancing to buy a larger deal in a larger market.

BUILDING A TEAM

When you are trying to get your first self storage deal or you're trying to flip it to build a portfolio, you need to build a team around you. You need this for deal flow—accountants, lenders, and brokers. You also need legal and financing people. You have to circle the people around you to get the deal done.

Then there's the second side: operations. You still have legal, accounting, mentors, management companies, vendors, and the people who are doing the day-to-day operation of those assets. They are all part of your team—you will have vendors for everything from technology to landscaping. We use Basecamp, a team communication and management app, to keep all those people on the same page. We meet with the finance team and the attorneys quarterly, to make sure everything is going right. Surround yourself with the right people, and you'll find the right deal and you'll manage it right too.

BUILDING YOUR EMPIRE

Here are my business strategies for domination in self storage.

The Concept of Franchising

The concept of franchising is really what I'm talking about in creating that repeatable process to add value to the facilities you buy—to get the look and feel you want.

In order to grow in real estate and build a self storage business that was dominating and had lots of assets, I needed two things:

1. I needed to be able to compound—to repeat my returns. I want to take my returns from one asset, put it into a another and repeat the growth of returns, and put it into another.

    My compounding is done through a value-add strategy. I always buy underperforming assets and apply my process to bring them up to a higher performance to generate that return—by increasing *income* and lowering *risk*. I lower my risk by buying underperforming assets with a known upside. That creates a greater margin of safety.

2. I needed to either recover my invested capital or save more. After I increase the value, I can either refinance or pull out that higher income to invest in another asset, and do it again.

If I get a 5% return, compounding is going to be slow. I wanted to do it a lot faster. For all of our assets, we have 100-plus % return in and capital out within three to four years, and those returns are infinite from then on. That's the goal.

That only works if you have a process to do it. My process was my management company.

The reason why it needs to feel like a franchise is simple: it needs to be systematic. There needs to be processes and systems. If not, you can't grow.

> *The processes and systems are what I think of as an FS—a **franchise system** that separates your time from your income.*

I'm not suggesting you buy a franchise. I'm suggesting you create a business that's like one.

That allows you to compound your return. In order to do this, I created Bitterroot Holdings. This became my wealth vehicle. It created the look and the feel of my storage facilities. It's repeated to make the value and the income to go up. It also lowers my risk, because the asset is not dependent on me.

The value of the asset should not be tied to the person who's running it. If you leave, the value could go with you. If it's not tied to you, the value goes up. The more you do it, the better you become at repeating that process.

READY TO GO? GET STARTED!

I hope you are inspired to take a step toward financial freedom by using what this book teaches you, along with the other resources I've provided, to invest in the self storage industry. It has changed my personal life and my financial life, and it can change yours. Join the Self Storage Income Facebook or Instagram groups, visit my YouTube channel and website SelfStorageIncome.com, and start learning how it works.

One of the great things about self storage is that it's scalable from very small assets in small markets to very large ones in large markets. You can choose what you are comfortable with and that helps you meet your goals.

The most important thing is to get started! Reach out and let us know about your journey. Never stop learning and improving.